The Globalization of Chinese Companies

STRATEGIES FOR CONQUERING INTERNATIONAL MARKETS

The Globalization of Chinese Companies

STRATEGIES FOR CONQUERING INTERNATIONAL MARKETS

Arthur Yeung
Katherine Xin
Waldemar Pfoertsch
Shengjun Liu

WILEY

John Wiley & Sons (Asia) Pte Ltd

Other Wiley Editorial Offices

John Wiley & Sons, 111 River Street, Hoboken, NJ 07030, USA
John Wiley & Sons, The Atrium, Southern Gate, Chichester, West Sussex,
P0198SQ, United Kingdom
John Wiley & Sons (Canada) Ltd., 5353 Dundas Street West, Suite 400, Toronto,
Ontario, M9B 6HB, Canada
John Wiley & Sons Australia Ltd, 42 McDougall Street, Milton, Queensland 4064,
Australia
Wiley-VCH, Boschstrasse 12, D-69469 Weinheim, Germany

Library of Congress Cataloging-in-Publication Data

ISBN 978-0-470-82878-6 (Hardcover)
ISBN 978-0-470-82880-9 (e-PDF)
ISBN 978-0-470-82879-3 (e-Mobi)
ISBN 978-0-470-82881-6 (e-Pub)

Typeset in 11/13 point, New Baskerville by MPS Limited a Macmillan Company,
Chennai, India

Printed in Singapore by Saik Wah Press Pte Ltd
10 9 8 7 6 5 4 3 2 1

Contents

Acknowledgments

The book is based on a book first published in Chinese under the title 鲜花与荆棘:探寻中国企业全球化之路.

Special thanks go to various colleagues and members of the faculty of CEIBS who helped us make this book available in English. In particular, we would like to thank the Management Committee of CEIBS for funding this research project, and Nancy Dai, one of our core research team members, for conducting extensive interviews and analyzing the huge amount of data. We are also grateful to Victory Zeshi for undertaking additional analyses.

Thanks go to Lena Hong Ye and Chrystal Xie for translating chapters of this book, Elise Chai and Marion Park for continuous improvements on the text, and Henry Han for providing us with updated data and organizational support.

Preface

In the first half of 2010, the Chinese economy became the world's second-largest in gross domestic product (GDP) terms, behind only that of the United States. In 2009, China also became the largest exporting nation and is striving to consolidate this position into the future. Now more than ever, with the globalization of the world economy, the game is being played on the largest potential playground.

In the last 50 years, numerous companies have entered the global market and changed the market landscape in their home countries and around the world. After World War II, U.S. firms took the lead, with European companies following soon after. In the 1970s, Japanese consumer-electronics and auto companies entered the lucrative markets of the industrialized world. In the '80s, Korean companies followed and became serious competitors to new entrants and established players alike. Now, Chinese companies are using their competitive advantages to establish themselves as global players.

The subject of globalization, particularly for Chinese companies, contains many issues worthy of analytical research: Why do companies want globalization? How can they position themselves in the globalized economy? What paths are available to them and which paths are more suitable for specific businesses to follow? What kind of globalization fits the organization's capabilities, and how can they create the necessary capabilities quickly and effectively?

Facing these complex issues, firms in China and around the world may easily become blinkered in their thinking; for example, seeing only the benefits of globalization while ignoring the costs.

They may only see the opportunities and forget to examine the scope and strength of their capabilities. We have found that many experts and scholars indulge in cheering success and criticizing failure, but fail to provide constructive solutions. They introduce the best practices of multinational companies without providing systematic analysis and reflection.

In 2009, the number of Chinese companies listed in the Global Fortune 500 list increased from 34 to 43 (see Appendix 9), and their revenue growth was impressive. However, coupled with the gains, there were also pains that few people know about. In fact, very little is known about how China has managed to ascend to the position it occupies today. But one thing is certain: there were many hardships along the way.

The purpose of this book is to shed light on the current situation of Chinese firms and to help Chinese entrepreneurs who want to undertake the challenges of globalization. We offer a thorough analysis of the current developments in this area; help aspiring candidates to develop a systematic approach; and help them to avoid errors in their thinking by providing a "navigation map" and a set of practical tools and instruments for managing the task of globalization.

This book is designed to provide a systematic and pragmatic approach to global expansion and competition for Chinese entrepreneurs and is based on both clear frameworks and detailed case studies. We believe that the book will be of practical benefit to Chinese senior executives facing the challenges of both global expansion and competition, and to managers, scholars, and students around the world who are interested in understanding how firms in China are striving to emerge in the global arena.

At the end of the book, we provide a self-assessment questionnaire covering all of the issues raised in these pages (see Appendix 10), something that can be utilized as a practical reference to the content. Immediately following, we provide an action plan (Appendix 11) which gives the reader/manager an opportunity to assess the current situation of their company in the context of going global. This tool has already helped to focus the strategic discussion within many companies in the course of going global. It is also available through the authors in Chinese/English and they will gladly assist with the interpretation of the results.

We firmly believe that the globalization of Chinese firms in the twenty-first century will be one of the most noteworthy events in the development of the world economy, and sincerely hope that this book will be helpful in contributing toward the rise of China's own "Sony and Samsung."

ARTHUR YEUNG
KATHERINE XIN
WALDEMAR PFOERTSCH
SHENGJUN LIU
SHANGHAI, 2010

1

Reaching Out

China is a sleeping giant. Let her sleep, for when she wakes she will shake the world.

Napoleon Bonaparte, 1803

China's position in the world economy has changed since the economic crises of 2008 and 2009. It is no longer simply perceived as the "production workshop of the world" and provider of cheap goods to the industrialized world. It is now recognized as the biggest holder of U.S. government bonds and a possible engine for global economic recovery. Without a doubt, China maintained its economic growth in this difficult time not only with the help of huge government stimulus packages but also with the strong commitment of Chinese entrepreneurs who have ambitions to be successful in the home market and beyond.[1]

Five years ago, very few consumers outside China had heard of the home-appliance producer Haier or the computer brand Lenovo. Today, they are sold successfully in the United States, Europe, and elsewhere. For years, Chinese companies have been producing shoes, toys, light bulbs, consumer electronics, and much more on behalf of foreign brands. Many Chinese homegrown brands can be found in Asia, the Middle East, Africa, and Latin America. More than 700,000 passenger cars, light trucks, and heavy trucks were sold overseas in 2008, with car manufacturer Chery leading the way. But it is not only in consumer products that China offers competitive goods at low prices; it also produces industrial goods such as heavy construction equipment (Sany, Zoomlion, and Tengzheng, for example), ships and containers, heavy machinery, and mining equipment, and even airplanes.[2] The newly formed Commercial Aircraft Corporation of China Ltd. (COMAC) received 280 orders (including 25 from GE Commercial Aviation Services) for its first ARJ21 medium-range jet, and has plans to deliver 20 of its new mid-size (190-seat) C919 to Western and Chinese customers in 2016. Also, China has become one of the fastest-growing aviation markets, with more than 200 million passengers in 2009 and projected annual growth of more than 7.8 percent for the next 20 years (see Appendix 1). While the airline industry suffered in other countries in the aftermath of the economic crisis, Chinese competitors strengthened their position and are expanding aggressively.[3]

In the 1980s, Japanese companies plunged into what was referred to as the "buying the entire United States" spree,[4] which saw the Wall Street Building, Rockefeller Center, and other U.S. landmark buildings swept up in its momentum. To the indignation of some Americans, Japanese companies acquired CBS and other industries that were part of the country's cultural identity. Since the start of the twenty-first century, China has been doing the same. It is widely reported that Chinese firms have been actively engaged in overseas M&As to the tune of US$0.2 billion in 2002, and US$5.28 billion in 2005. These numbers continue to increase; according to statistics provided by the Chinese Ministry of Commerce, the amount in 2008 reached US$20.5 billion.[5] The TCL Group was widely known as the "pioneer" in aggressive overseas acquisition to realize its global aspirations. Many other companies, such as Lenovo, CNOOC, SAIC, and BenQ, undertook similar initiatives from 2000–08 and, most recently, Geely made a deal with Ford to acquire Volvo.

Burning Passion

In September 2002, the TCL Group, one of China's largest appliance companies, announced that it had acquired the substantial assets the Germany company Schneider Electronics AG for €8.2 million (US$8 million), creating a European production base for color televisions. The acquisition was cleverly made to bypass the

European Union's aggressive anti-dumping regulation against Chinese electrical-appliance firms. Few realized that this was just a warm-up for a series of overseas acquisitions by the TCL Group. In July 2003, TCL chairman Li Dongsheng formally announced the Group's "Dragon and Tiger Plan" to establish two competitive businesses in global markets (dragons) and three leading businesses inside China (tigers). This plan became the TCL-style "Great Leap toward Globalization."

Later that year, TCL announced a joint venture with the French electronics giant Thomson (the originator of color-TV sets and the owner of more than 34,000 TV patents), with TCL owning 67 percent of the new entity (TTE). Remarkably, sales of TTE's color TV sets reached 18.5 million units in 2003, which established the company as the leader in this field and thrust TCL onto the world stage just 10 years after its entrance into the highly competitive color-TV market. In April 2004, TCL and another French company, Alcatel, announced the establishment of a joint venture that would engage in the production and sales operations of mobile phones. TCL injected €55 million (US$67.7 million) for a 55 percent shareholding. With this, TCL became the world's seventh-largest mobile-phone manufacturer. Through the acquisition, TCL acquired core 3G technologies in network and wireless access systems. It thus became one of the few Chinese manufacturers of mobile phones with a core technology, which meant that it not only bought market share, but also acquired capabilities to prepare for the future.

Surging Forward

TCL was not the only one to make the "Great Leap Forward." In February 2003, BOE Technology Group Co. Ltd. announced the acquisition of the Hydis Company, the Hyundai Group's TFT-LCD business (the key component for flat-panel screens), in a transaction valued at about US$380 million, a record for a Chinese acquisition at that time.

In October the following year, the Chinese auto-industry leader, SAIC, spent US$500 million in acquiring a 48.92 percent stake of South Korea's Ssangyong Motor—the first overseas acquisition in the Chinese automobile industry. In May 2005, when the century-old British MG Rover company declared bankruptcy, with an attendant layoff of more than 6,000 workers, SAIC and the Nanjing Automobile Corporation stepped in to rescue the company. The latter bought the assets of MG Rover, including the MG and Austin brands, for £53 million (US$101.1 million).[6] Before Rover's bankruptcy, SAIC had spent £67 million (US$127.8 million) on the purchase of part of the intellectual-property rights of the Rover 25 and Rover 27 models, which were introduced to the Chinese market in 2007 and 2008 as Roewe 550 and 750, respectively. Ironically, in 2007 Nanjing Automobile was acquired by SAIC, with support from the Shanghai and Nanjing governments, giving SAIC access to the precious MG and Austin Martin brands.

On December 24, 2004, the Lenovo Group gave itself a Christmas present by buying IBM's worldwide PC business at a price of US$1.75 billion. The new Lenovo surged forward to become one of the global top three, increasing its global PC market share from 2.3 percent to 8.3 percent on the back of revenues of US$13 billion and sales of 14 million PCs. This was a dream come true for Lenovo, whose market share in Europe and the U.S. had been close to zero before the acquisition. Yang Yuanqing, chairman of the new Lenovo, admitted that, when the possibility had been first raised by IBM a few years earlier: "I felt that it was just like the Arabian Nights."[7]

In January 2005, the smallest of China's three major oil companies, CNOOC, offered as much as US$13 billion to acquire the ninth-largest U.S. oil company, Unocal, and subsequently increased the offer to US$18.5 billion. The American public became unsettled with fears that national security would be threatened by Communist China's offer. Members of Congress were suspicious of the government ownership of CNOOC and exerted pressure against the acquisition, preventing the deal from going through.

As early as 2002, the Haier Group had spent US$14 million in acquiring the Greenwich Savings Bank building—a New York landmark—as its North American headquarters. Haier was less successful, however, in its subsequent attempts to acquire U.S. companies. In June 2005, Haier announced a bid of US$1.28 billion for the veteran U.S. appliance firm Maytag, and was turned down. At the 2005 Globalization Forum of Chinese firms, Haier Group CEO Zhang Ruimin pointed out that "Haier's internationalization is at the gateway, blocked by foreign competitors. If we pass this obstacle, we will make great success, otherwise we will become martyrs."[8]

In June 2005, BenQ acquired the global mobile-phone business of Siemens and emerged as the world's fourth-largest mobile-phone brand. In the process of the acquisition, BenQ did not spend a single cent, but rather received a "dowry" of €250 million (US$454.2 million) from Siemens, scoring a big bargain compared to TCL and Lenovo's costs of their acquisitions. The newly formed BenQ-Siemens mobile communications subsidiary went on to win the most prestigious iF design awards in Germany's "red dot" competition.[9]

In August 2007, six months after announcing its acquisition of the Philips mobile-phone business, China Electronics Corporation (CEC) started to run the business with a team from Philips. This was the first time that Philips had enfranchised its brand to a third party. CEC also announced its intention to work closely with retailers and explore overseas markets, with an expected investment of RMB100 million (US$13.2 million).

On October 25, 2007, the Industrial and Commercial Bank of China (ICBC) announced its purchase of 20 percent of the Standard Bank of South Africa for US$5.6 billion in cash, the biggest foreign acquisition by a Chinese commercial bank yet. According to an ICBC report, it gained a US$1.213 billion cash dividend and US$589 million capital bonus from the Standard Bank in 2008, an annual rate of return on investment of 7.7 percent. By the end of March 2009, the ICBC and Standard Bank had completed nine out of the 65 joint projects based on the premise of their closer relationship.[10]

China Merchants Bank, one of China's most innovative banks, acquired 53.12 percent of Hong Kong's Wing Lung Bank for HK$19.3 billion (US$2.5 billion). In 2008, the Sinosteel Corporation, one of China's biggest steel companies, purchased the U.S.-based Midwest Corporation. This deal was adjudged the "Best Deal" and "Best Requisition Deal" of the year, respectively, by *Finance Asia* and *Assets*.

In 2008, China Metallurgical Group Corp. signed an agreement with Cape Lambert Iron Ore Ltd., an Australian company, to buy its flagship iron-ore project for A$400 million (US$376.6 million). In July 2009, it sealed a deal with Waratah Coal Inc., another Australian company, to fund up to 70 percent of a A$5.15 billion (US$4.2 billion) venture project and take a 10 percent stake.

In February 2009, Shenzhen Zhongjin Lingnan Nonfemet Co. (SZLN), a Shenzhen state-owned mining business, invested A$45 million (US$ 28.6 million) into Perilya, an ailing Perth-based metal mining company, and acquired a 50.1 percent stake in the business. As a result of the deal, in which it became the first Chinese metal company to acquire a controlling stake in an Australian mining business, SZLN is now China's largest zinc-lead producer. This move, seen by some as "the smartest deal with the most favorable price of any Australian resource acquisition by a Chinese mining company over the last two years,"[11] is very significant for SZLN and its "going global" initiative. On May 26, 2009, the state-owned Guangdong Rising Nonferrous Metals Group, SZLN's parent company, signed a deal with Pan Australian Resources Ltd. to become its largest shareholder, with the purchase of a 19.9 percent stake worth A$140 million (US$102.1 million). This is Rising's second acquisition in Australia.

In May 2009, Haier announced that it planned to acquire a 20 percent stake in Fisher & Paykel—New Zealand's largest home-appliance maker—and become its largest shareholder. The deal gives Haier exclusive rights to sell Fisher & Paykel's home appliances in China and Fisher & Paykel reciprocal rights to sell Haier products in Australia and New Zealand.

In June 2009, GM and Sichuan Tengzhong Heavy Industrial Machinery, a private Chinese firm, made an initial agreement concerning the latter's purchase of GM's famous Hummer brand.[12] On the same day, Shanshan, a Ningbo-based Chinese menswear brand, announced that it had reached an agreement with Australia Heron Resources Ltd. for a 70 percent interest in a joint development of the Yerilla nickel-cobalt project. As part of the agreement, Shanshan has proposed to acquire 12.045 million Heron shares, or 4.99 percent of the Australian company's outstanding share capital. By giving Shanshan a foothold in the raw-materials supply chain, the deal has secured the company's further development.

The Collective Ambition

For decades, the economy of China has maintained a growth rate faster than that of any other nation. From 1978–2008, China's average GDP growth rate was 9.83 percent.[13] The growth rate of its leading companies was even higher. However, as local challengers matured and foreign companies entered, industry competition became much more severe. In order to survive, many Chinese companies applied a price-war strategy to maintain market share.

The purpose behind Chinese companies going global is not simply about winning a global market; it is also about technology, brand, and sales channels. Most Chinese companies are at the bottom of the Stan Shih[14] Smiling Curve (see Figure 1.1). For example, the Japanese zipper-producer YKK earns US$15 for one meter of its zippers, while Chinese competitors earn only RMB0.7 (US$0.1 in 2008) per meter.

When TCL decided to acquire Thomson, the company considered the move a "can't miss" opportunity to turn itself into a real global player. This kind of short-cut mindset was not uncommon during that time. Lenovo and BenQ also had this mindset, with different degrees of disappointment. For example, in 2002 Changhong, then China's leading TV manufacturer, exported televisions and DVD players to the value of US$780 million to the United States. However, while it was enjoying great success overseas, its competitor, APEX, snared the domestic market. In the end, Changhong lost US$472 million and suffered dramatically. This failure could be attributed to a lack of global experience and also to impatience on the part of Chinese companies' to globalize.

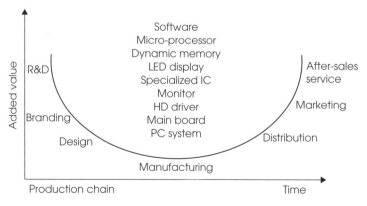

Figure 1.1   The Stan Shih Smiling Curve[15]

Things to Remember

The news that TCL had taken control of the valuable RCA TV brand in November 2003 caused a ripple in global consciousness, as did the sale of IBM's PC business to Lenovo in December 2004. Unfortunately, while China's acquisitions draw headlines, the outcomes are not always positive.

For many established names in the electronics business, TCL was a quiet assassin. Founded in South China in 1982 to make magnetic tape in response to the mainland's appetite for music from Hong Kong and Taiwan, TCL became a huge force in the television manufacturing industry, where its modestly priced, mid-tier product outperformed established Western competitors.

In spite of its great expectations of becoming the largest television manufacturer in the world, the iconic deal that led to the creation of TCL-Thomson Electronics (TTE) quickly turned to disappointment. The reality was that an increase in size and becoming a household brand name did not spare it from harsh competitive pressures. In its first year, the joint venture lost HK$599 million (US$77 million), followed by another HK$1.5 billion (US$220 million) in the first three-quarters of that year. Overall, almost half of its shareholders' equity quickly disappeared, and the value of TTE's shares on the Hong Kong stock exchange collapsed.

While TTE's business suffered all over the world, there were sharp differences between regions. Profits decreased minimally in China, where TTE had a particularly strong franchise, and in other developing countries, where manufacturers cleverly ship disassembled televisions to be then put together by local companies. In the United States, where both TCL and Thomson operated, the joint venture came close to breaking even, but in Europe, Thomson's home market, it was disastrous; TTE lost €159 million (US$203 million) on sales of €328 million (US$419 million) in 2006. In October that year, TTE announced that most of its European operations would be shrunk, sold, closed, or returned, including a factory in Poland and an expensive distribution network. Even the Thomson brand name would have largely disappeared within two years. TTE would instead concentrate on producing TV sets to be sold by other companies, with none of the cost of support and distribution that a brand requires. Even better, supervision for this kind of business would be based in China.

A big problem was that both TCL and Thomson focused on clunky old models that used cathode-ray tubes, despite the fact that the market favored flat screens. But even that did not completely explain TTE's troubles, since many flat-screen panel manufacturers were not doing particularly well either. Flat-screen manufacturing facilities cost billions of dollars, and in return for this investment producers often watched the price of their product drop by as much as 10 percent a month as a result of heavy competition. With this rapid fall in the price of flat-screen panels, TTE believed the key element for success was not just technology (the panel) but also the control of inventory. A conventional TV set took 90 days to make and send to America, by which time the price would have fallen. TTE wanted to shorten that to less than 30 days, including the 20 days it took the TVs to cross the Pacific. Boats used to be seen as time-wasting transport, but were regarded as floating warehouses holding products while sales were arranged. "TTE has to have a really good year," Aaron Tong, vice-president of TTE Strategy Planning, commented in 2006. "If we stumble, we will be gone forever."

Lenovo has experienced similar hardships. In 2009, while Lenovo was busy with integration, its rivals enlarged their market share globally, resulting in the biggest loss ever for Lenovo in the last quarter of 2008. The company changed its CEO three times in the period from 2005 to 2009. Meanwhile, Acer became the second-largest PC producer in the world, further sabotaging Lenovo's ambition to become a global leader.

The financial industry also faced disappointments. In October 2007 and December 2008, China Minsheng Bank invested RMB889 million (US$130 million) in UCBH, an American bank focusing on Chinese customers in California. In return, it obtained 9.9 percent of UCBH shares. When UCBH went bankrupt in November 2009, Minsheng Bank lost almost all of its investment. When the stock price of Fortis, Belgium's leading bank, quickly dropped in 2007, Ping An took a gamble in the recession market and spent €1.8 billion (US$2.6 billion) to buy 4.18 percent of Fortis shares, thus becoming the largest shareholder. However, Fortis didn't survive the financial crisis and Ping An lost most of its investment in this bet.

Questions to Ask

Given the degree of frustration encountered by Chinese companies, we should put some thought into exactly what their problems are. Are they failing because of poor economic strength, limited opportunities, or a lack of management know-how? From our research, we conclude that the failure of most Chinese companies going global could be generalized as follows:

- They have only a partial understanding of globalization.
- They lack sufficient analysis and thought toward globalization.
- They lack the organizational capabilities required for globalization.
- They do not prepare well for opportunities that present themselves.

On a more positive note, there are a number of Chinese companies that have achieved relative success in their globalization plans. These include Haier, Huawei, Chery, China State Construction Engineering Corporation (CSCEC), China Ocean Shipping (Group) Company (COSCO), Baosteel, First Automobile Works (FAW), Minemetals, China Mobile, Aluminum Corporation of China Limited (CHALCO), China Petroleum & Chemical Corporation (Sinopec), and Sinochem.

As one of China's largest appliance companies, the Haier Group has been stepping up its efforts to build a global brand that stands comparison with Samsung and Sony. Haier already has a global manufacturing presence, including North American headquarters in New York and plants in South Carolina and Italy. Its washing machines and refrigerators are sold across the U.S. in chains such as Wal-Mart, as well as in Europe. Haier has also created some popular products, including a mini-fridge sized to fit a six-pack of beer, and a pizza box that has become a hit with college students. Such products and an international distribution network have helped Haier become a top contender in the race among Chinese companies to build global brands. While it doesn't yet have the strongest brand name, the company has continued to expand its product range. In addition to household appliances, it produces high-end products such as flat-screen TVs, computers, and mobile phones. Now that its product range is starting to look more like Samsung's showroom, Haier wants to re-create its Korean rival's successful image transformation from cheap Sony knock-offs to high-tech powerhouse. After several months of searching, Haier chose former Motorola marketer Larry Rinaldi to head its global marketing. In 2007, Rinaldi, an American with international marketing and agency experience and a strong Chinese background, was appointed to the new position of global chief brand officer. In 2008, Haier hired Philip Carmichael as president of Asia Pacific to help China's ambitious appliances giant to create a global brand.

Although Haier's global brand-building effort has not been entirely successful, it is deserving of respect and praise for its unique strategy in going out, entering into, and positioning itself at the high end of the market.

In addition to Haier, there are 36 Chinese companies listed in "The 2009 BCG 100 New Global Challengers" published by the Boston Consulting Group. These companies conducted 43 outbound M&As from January 2005 to mid-2008.[16] Therefore, we are confident that more and more Chinese companies have the potential to go global.

What is a Truly Global Firm?

There are three sets of criteria by which to evaluate whether a company could be recognized as a global company. First, a global company should be able to compete in a global market, which can be seen from its market share and sales volume in the global market. Second, a global company must be able to leverage resources globally, including its sales and distribution channels, production facilities, R&D network, and employee base around the world. This set of criteria could truly assess the extent to which the global company utilizes global resources. Third, a global company has the ability to organize and manage its business operations on a global scale. Resource globalization alone is not enough; resources should be effectively integrated to fulfill their global advantages. To seize opportunities in worldwide markets, the company should be supported by global organizational capabilities, including global leadership, global mindset, global organizational structure, a balance between global integration and local adaptation, speedy feedback and information-sharing mechanisms, and successful experiences. The degree to which a company can be considered globalized can be likened to a tree (see Figure 1.2). The fruits it bears are its global sales and market share; the trunk is its utilization of resources on a global scale; and its roots are its organizational capability.[17]

Chinese high-tech, consumer electronics, and industrial products companies are outgrowing the domestic market, improving their productivity, and rigorously defending their domestic markets against

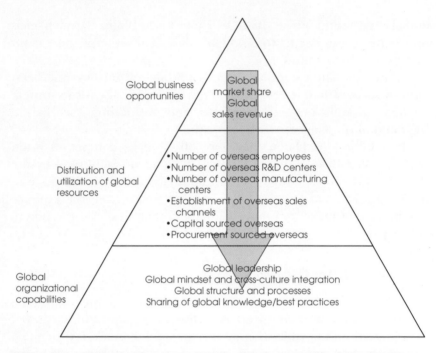

Figure 1.2   Globalization Tree: Depth of a Company's Globalization

foreign challengers. But our research also shows that most of these companies will have difficulty replicating these gains in other countries, where they must meet and accommodate the needs of very different customers. To do this, they must attract talent familiar with local business environments, compete with entrenched local competitors, and establish a brand-new sales and marketing presence.

Scale has spurred productivity and helps Chinese companies to dominate the market in their homeland. However, to secure continued growth, companies must push into overseas markets, which require different skills and higher expenditures on marketing, research, and labor. Before fully committing their resources to global expansion, our research suggests that Chinese companies have to answer three questions.

First, they must clarify their global aspiration, which relates to the why, what, and where of their globalization journey. Why go global? Is it for resource utilization or market expansion? What products/services should they go global in? Is it R&D, procurement, manufacturing, or sales? Where to go global: developing countries or developed countries? Paradoxically, many Chinese firms overestimate the benefits of globalization and underestimate its costs. For example, as Chinese technology companies grow in the domestic market, the ratio between R&D costs and revenue falls, since R&D expenses are spread across a rising revenue base. Once a company expands globally, the trend can reverse abruptly. Globalizing companies also face cost increases for marketing because they must build brand recognition and learn the ways of unfamiliar consumers, and for labor as they begin hiring talent outside their own low-wage domestic market.

Second, companies need to think carefully about the right path to follow in pursuing globalization. Generally, there are three available options for companies going global: internal organic growth; strategic alliances; and mergers and acquisitions. While technology businesses are in the vanguard of China's foray into global markets, a company wishing to follow pioneers such as Lenovo and the telecom giant Huawei must judge which is the most viable path to take given their current management knowhow and resources. This choice of path is often tied to their current stage of globalization. In the initial stage, companies often pursue strategic alliances; for example, through trading firms, overseas distributors, or OEM business. As they become more experienced, they can pursue organic growth to establish overseas operations themselves or acquire overseas companies to accelerate the process.

Third, these Chinese companies also need to assess the readiness of their global organizational capability to go global and to devise strategies to build such capabilities quickly. Despite impressive accomplishments by Chinese manufacturers in many aspects, our analysis shows that most Chinese companies lack this capability as a result of their short history and insufficient exposure to global operations.

This is the same challenge that confronted Japanese and Korean companies such as Sony and Samsung in the 1960s and 1970s; their success in meeting the challenge speaks for itself. The key questions to think through in undergoing the globalization process are summarized in the diagnostic framework presented in Figure 1.3.

Figure 1.3   Diagnostic Framework of Globalization

Endnotes

1. For more historic explanations, see Martin Jacques, *When China Rules the World: The End of the Western World and the Birth of a New Global Order* (London: Penguin Press, 2009).
2. Waldemar Pfoertsch, "China's Multinational Future—China is building its corporate giants in many different ways," *China International Business* 4, April 20, 2010, Shanghai.
3. Interview with Air China Chairman Kong Dong, *Flight International*, April 2009.
4. Katsuro Sakoh, "Japanese Investment in the US: Creating Jobs and Narrowing the Trade Deficit," *Asian Studies Body-grounder* 44, The Heritage Foundation, April 16, 2006.
5. "Chinese buyouts overseas" (in Chinese) at http://finance.people.com.cn/GB/70392/9557183.html. Accessed July 2009.
6. Chen Zijia, "SAIC and NAC Will Probably Cooperate on Rover Project," *Beijing Business Today*, April 20, 2007.
7. Zhou Jiansen, "Lenovo Acquires PC Division from IBM with US$1.25 billion," *Beijing Daily*, December 9, 2004.
8. Internal materials distributed by China Group Companies Promotion Association, May 2005.
9. Wikipedia. http://en.wikipedia.org/wiki/BenQ-Siemens. Accessed June 2009.

10. "ICBC in Good Cooperation with Standard Bank of South Africa" at http:// www.icbc.com.cn/icbc/工行风貌/工行快讯/工商银行与南非标准银行战略合作渐入佳境.htm. 2009. Accessed July 2009.

11. Chen Jialu, "Australian Acquisition Proves Rich Seam for SZLN," *China Daily*, July 7, 2009.

12. The deal was finally stopped by government intervention.

13. OECD: Economic Outlook NO.86-China, Paris, September 2009.

14. Dr. Stan Shih is the co-founder of the pan Acer Group. Dr. Shih has led Acer to become one of the world's leading PC companies and he is recognized around the globe for his achievements in brand-business building, and for his renowned Smiling Curve business model for the high-tech industry. Dr. Shih began his career at Unitron Industrial Corp. in 1971 and successfully designed, developed, and commercialized Taiwan's first desktop calculator.

15. Smiling Curve is an illustration of the value-adding potential of different components of the value chain in an IT-related manufacturing industry. The concept was first proposed by Stan Shih around 1992. According to Shih's observation, in the personal computer industry, both ends of the value chain command higher value added to the product than the middle part of the value chain. If this phenomenon is presented in a graph with a Y-axis for value-added and an X-axis for value chain (stage of production), the resulting curve appears like a "smile." Based on this vision, Acer has adopted a business strategy to recreate itself from a manufacturer into a company that focuses on global marketing of branded PC-related products and services. Meanwhile, Acer has also invested aggressively in R&D to develop innovative technology. The concept later became widely cited in Asia to describe the distribution of value-adding potential in various industries to justify business strategies aimed at higher value-adding activities.

16. Boston Consulting Group, "The 2009 BCG 100 New Global Challengers," Boston 2009, and also available at: http://www.bcg.com/impact_expertise/ publications/files/The 2009_BCG_100_New_Global_Challengers_Jan_ 2009. pdf. 2009. Accessed April 2010.

17. The ability and capacity of an organization to perform certain tasks based on its human resources, cultures, organization design, core organizing processes, and information/knowledge sharing. See also, Dave Ulrich and Dale Lake, "Organizational capability: creating competitive advantage," *Academy of Management Executive* 5(1), 1991: 77–92.

CHAPTER 2

Realities and Aspirations

Globalization made GE a company looking for global opportunities, not only for selling products or purchasing, but also for intelligence capital, global talents, and great ideas.

Jack Welch

It may be an exaggeration to say that companies have no future without becoming globalized. However, it is a fact that multinational companies are spreading their wings all over the world at a rapid pace; they will soon become the norm. Currently, 80 percent of all global Fortune 500 companies have their business in China, and foreign direct investment (FDI) has been a key factor supporting China's high economic growth. As a result, more and more Chinese companies are becoming involved in the global value chain without even trying. For example, Wal-Mart imported goods worth US$32.1 billion from China in 2007 alone.[1] So many companies seem to be in such a hurry to globalize, one has to wonder if they are aware of what is driving them on. In fact, many European and American companies go into the Chinese market although they gain little profit. Such behavior prompted Jack Welch, the former CEO of GE to question, "Is China for everyone?"[2]

National Competitive Advantages

There are different theories proposed by Western researchers regarding what motivates companies to pursue globalization. One of the most influential of these is the "national competitive advantages theory" proposed by Michael E. Porter, who maintains that different countries have different competitive advantages.[3] The determinants of national advantage are based on four factors:

- factor condition (abundant supply of labor force and selected natural resources)
- demand condition (high domestic market scale and increasing customer-demand characteristic)
- related and supporting industry (availability and clustering of suppliers)
- corporate strategy, structure, and rivalry (strong degree of domestic market competition through local and foreign firms).

Different national companies have different characteristics, with respective advantages and disadvantages. Japan and Germany, for example, pursue innovation and quality, partially as a result of their lack of basic resources. Companies can take advantage of their country's conditions to develop competitive advantage during globalization. For example, China International Marine Containers (Group) Ltd. (CIMC) has become a market leader because it had the foresight to see that China would attain a leading position in international trade (see Appendix 2 and 3). Some nations take advantage of other nations' competitive advantage to further their own interests. For example, more and more Western companies are selecting China as their manufacturing base and India as their software R&D center.

The Value of Globalization

Globalization has changed the competitive parameters of companies in many respects, such as higher requirements in production scale, global channels and vanguard technology. Globalization removes boundaries, making it increasingly difficult for companies to compete solely within their national territories. Competitive advantage can be elevated by a company's ability to further utilize resources and market opportunities beyond national borders. For example, at the end of the 1960s, Otis, the world's leading manufacturer/installer/maintainer of elevators, escalators, and moving walkways (with US$12.9 billion in revenues in 2008, 80 percent of which were generated outside the United States), found that the European elevator market was dominated by many local companies, and most of the multinational companies also localized their business. Otis decided to change the status quo by applying standardized design to cut cost, and thus found its competitive edge. Today, Otis is a major contributor of profit for its holding company, United Technologies Corporation.

Different companies have different motives, goals, and strategic emphases for going global and these may change at different stages of the process. However, the ultimate goal of globalization for everyone is to create greater value through the changes in different drivers and variables, as illustrated in Figure 2.1.

The profit of many global companies comes from the difference between the selling price in industrialized markets and the production cost in other locations. Globalization can help increase profit through the following means:

Increased sales (bigger volume): A company can go abroad for a larger market in hopes of increased sales. Many global companies grew from small and local entities. Wal-Mart, for example, started its business in 1945 in Bentonville, a small town in the U.S., and

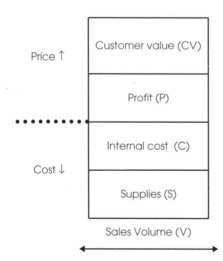

Figure 2.1   Value Creation through Globalization

became the biggest company in the world in only a few decades. The first overseas store was founded in Mexico in 1991 and by 2006, the company had grown to more than 2,700 retail outlets in 15 nations, with more than 1,500,000 employees. Starbucks began in Seattle and, since establishing its first overseas store in Tokyo in 1996, has spread worldwide in great numbers.

Globalized companies depend more on the global market than on their own, which they have generally outgrown after achieving a certain level of success. This is especially true for countries such as Japan and Korea, which have limited natural resources and a small local market. In such circumstances, the ability of local companies to globalize has brought economic success way beyond what is possible in their home markets. Originally, Toyota set up its overseas factory to avoid trade protectionism. In 1959, it set up its overseas manufacturing base in Brazil to follow local policy. It established its own privately owned company in the United States in 1988 and now has 52 factories in 26 countries. Other examples of successful globalization include Nestlé from Switzerland, Nokia from Finland, Ericsson from Sweden, and Novo Nordisk from Denmark.

Cost reductions through cheaper labor and other factors of production (lower costs of supply): Facing ongoing competition, the question of how to reduce costs becomes an important issue for many companies. Beyond making improvements to the efficiency of internal management, procuring low-cost labor and other factors of production (such as land) is another remarkably effective way to reduce costs. Many multinational corporations have set up factories in China to take advantage of China's cheap labor force. In 2008, the Italian luxury brand Ermenegildo Zegna entered into an agreement with the Wenzhou Xiameng Group to manufacture its clothes in China. Within China, intense competition among municipal governments to attract foreign direct investment has led many local governments to offer generous incentives in land provision, preferential tax rates, and subsidies to lure foreign companies. Lower costs play an important role in persuading foreign companies to move from coastal regions to inland China, where local governments are more concerned with maximizing GDP growth than with costly issues such as environmental protection.

Cost reductions through economies of scale (lower costs of supply and operation): This cost-reduction strategy seems to be working best for Chinese companies. Many Western companies have applied this principle in mass-produced products, but its effectiveness only became clearly visible through Asian consumer-electronics companies such as Panasonic, Sanyo, and Sony. Now, China's emerging dragons are winning shares across a wide spectrum of industries with this strategy. Consider a few examples: Galanz now supplies more than half of all microwave ovens sold in the global market; BYD is the world's second-largest maker of rechargeable batteries; CIMC, with a 55 percent global market share, dominates the world of shipping containers and is six times larger than its nearest international competitor; Shanghai Zhenhua Port Machinery Company (ZPMC) has a 54 percent share of the world market for harbor cranes (see Appendix 4); Pearl River Piano, which has gained 15 percent of the U.S. market (40 percent in upright pianos) in just five years, is the global volume leader, producing around 100,000 pianos every year; Wanxiang, the world's largest producer of universal joints, has established a fund to buy U.S. auto-components firms and has already made 18 acquisitions across four continents. The obvious benefits of increased scale are higher bargaining power in external procurement and lower overheads in internal operating costs.

Acquisition of critical resources (higher quality of supply): The globalized economy forces countries to compete for strategic resources. Where there is a large gap between supply and demand for valuable resources such as petroleum, timber, and iron ore, countries must go outside their boundaries to procure what they need. For this reason, the China National Offshore Oil Corporation (CNOOC) sought to buy American oil company Unocal for its rich oil and gas reserves. Similarly, Sinopec spent US$4.18 billion to buy Kazakhstan oil, and Baosteel paid US$118 million to get 98.4 percent of Peruvian iron ore. In 2004, Shanghai Anxin Floor invested some RMB100 million (US$15.87 million) to purchase a parcel of forest in Brazil covering 1,000 km^2 to secure supply of high-quality wood.

Capital and talent are also important resources in a broader sense. Trend Micro is a good example of improving competitive edge through integrating global resources.[4] It established a transnational organization with global centers in different parts of the world—a global financial center in Japan; a global R&D center in Taiwan; a global marketing center in the U.S.; and a global customer-support center in the Philippines—to capture high-quality, low-cost resources in those countries. Sha-steel is sensitive to the moves of global steel giants. In 2001, learning that ThyssenKrupp was to close its Phoenix factory, Sha-steel seized the opportunity to acquire its integrated production lines, with a production capacity of 6,500,000 tons, for €33.8 million (US$33.5 million). It then spent a year to move the 250,000-ton equipment (the largest industrial moving project in Europe since World War II) to China, increasing its total production capacity to 10,000,000 tons. Acquiring critical resources overseas enabled Sha-steel to upgrade both production capacity and capability and, in the process, to elevate itself into the ranks of Fortune 500 in 2009.

Acquiring know-how to increase customer value or reduce costs: Companies rely on cutting-edge know-how and innovation in such areas as product technologies, production processes, and management processes such as branding and customer services to create more value for their customers. The creation of customer value determines the price that they can ask/expect from their customers. Companies can best acquire such expertise and experience by reaching beyond their national boundaries. Indeed, one of the key reasons for many overseas acquisitions (for example, TCL's acquisition of Thomson's TV business or Lenovo's acquisition of IBM's PC business) is to gain immediate access to the technologies, patents, and management know-how of foreign companies. Companies can also improve their know-how by leveraging their global presence. For instance, an international company can apply the successful practices of one unit or region to other units or regions, multiplying the value creation to more clients in different parts of the world. For international Western companies, skills acquired in protecting intellectual property in China can be applied to other organizations in developing countries. As early as 1970, Harry Johnson[5] offered an interesting theory to explain the value of global expansion. He pointed out that expertise created by a company could be used in its branches abroad without increasing cost, while local companies have to spend more to acquire this expertise. The differences in competitive edge countries have also decide the features of knowledge acquisition. For example, many Chinese firms have set up R&D centers in the U.S. and other industrialized countries because this is the most developed consumer market in the world. As Akio Morita pointed out when Sony established the Advanced Video Technology Center in California in 1989: "If the R&D results of each branch's advantageous fields, such as digitals in the U.K., graphics and special effect technologies in the U.S., can be copied in others regions, the achievement of R&D activities will be magnified."[6] Sony had as many as 20 overseas R&D centers in the 1990s. Chinese companies which have established such centers overseas include the wind-turbine manufacturer Envision, and the acoustic-equipment company New Jialian, which have both set up R&D facilities in Denmark. More Chinese high-tech firms are following suit. Many of these centers are charged with the responsibility to catch up with market leaders. Currently, staffing levels in these centers are relatively small, with only a few (Huawei in Bangalore and Haier in the United States, for example) employing more than 500 people.[7]

Offering products/services to global customers (higher customer value): Following customers, especially key accounts, is another important reason for some companies to go global. Companies that fail to enter new markets with their clients risk losing not only orders, but also their long-term partnerships. The relationship between Delphi and GM is very typical. As an automotive-component supplier, Delphi was part of GM and is now in symbiosis with GM, following the latter into different markets. This practice is more commonplace in service industries. Logitech, the largest computer-mouse producer in the world, brought more than 30 long-term partners with it when it settled in Suzhou, a city neighboring Shanghai. Companies in the fields of finance, insurance, branding or advertising are required to provide "universal solutions" that serve their key clients in a globally integrated manner. IBM was working with more than 70 advertising agencies worldwide in 1993. Its CEO Louis Gerstner was surprised to find 18 versions of IBM advertisements appearing in one trade magazine, each different in design, wording and logo.[8] Subsequently, IBM entrusted its global advertising to Ogilvy which, with 359 branches in 100 countries, is able to offer the global service support its clients need. This helps to create higher value for its clients and enables them to command a higher price premium.

Reducing risks: According to Harry Markowitz's Portfolio Theory,[9] it is dangerous to put all your eggs in one basket. Diversification is an effective way to reduce risks. International companies can make a profit in emerging markets when developed markets are facing recession. This can be the case for Chinese companies going abroad. Beverage company Wahaha, for example, has gotten onto market shelves in the U.S. by selling its protein and vitamin drinks for children in Asian specialty stores. In 2008, Volkswagen's vehicle sales in China rose 12.5 percent to 1.04 million, which represented 16 percent of its global sales.[10] The vigorous growth of the Chinese auto market provided a new profit point for VW. Duerr AG is a global leader in auto-painting systems, with branches in 18 countries. Even as the European and American markets are shrinking, the company is able to profit from large orders from Chinese automakers. Moreover, when certain currencies appreciate, the company can reallocate some of its production to reduce costs. With this measure in place, Duerr's sales in 2008 reached €1.5 billion (US $2.1 billion).[11]

In summary, the ultimate objective of globalization is to achieve sustained profit by increasing sales volume, reducing costs of supply and internal management, and improving customer value. All these translate into lower costs and/or higher prices, which equal higher profit.

Targeting Business Activities to Globalize

Companies must have a clear understanding of their motives for globalization (to improve volume, costs, and/or price) in order to determine which parts of their business operation to globalize (see Figure 2.2).

Although R&D and product design are core departments, an increasing number of Asian companies are moving these functions to developed countries to access advanced technologies, while some Western companies are transferring their R&D departments to developing countries (such as China and India) to make use of high-quality, low-cost talent. The sophistication of the Internet and other communication technologies facilitates the interaction between R&D centers and headquarters around the globe.

Figure 2.2   Value Chain of Business Operation Activities

It is important that companies be aware of the necessity to protect their intellectual property when transferring R&D centers overseas, because developing countries are legally and culturally less sensitive to such issues. R&D with less technology content and peripheral product design can be moved overseas safely at the beginning to reduce risks. Developing countries such as China provide preferential policies to attract international R&D centers, since they cause less pollution and take less space than factories (see Figure 2.3). In addition, there is the positive spillover effect that can help developing countries to train their talent and upgrade their industrial structure.

Globalization enables the procurement of low-cost, high-quality raw materials, and helps international companies to realize scale effects in negotiations with suppliers. For instance, after acquiring Thomson's color TV business, TCL transferred the global procurement of some key components to China. IBM announced the relocation of its global procurement headquarters from New York to Shenzhen in October 2006. This was the first time that IBM had moved a department headquarters outside of the U.S. Subsequently, it entered into business relations with more than 3,000 suppliers in Asia. In 2005, IBM's procurement expenditure in the Asia-Pacific region was US$12 billion, accounting for 30 percent of its global procurement expenditure.

Among other things, globalization means finding the best places to locate manufacturing, operations, marketing, and services. For example, Trend Micro has located its customer-support center to the Philippines because of the trained, English-speaking labor available there; its finance center is in Japan because of the well-developed financial system and low interest rate; and its marketing center is located in the U.S. because of the advanced marketing knowledge, information software and high-tech systems available in that country. For a company seeking to increase its overseas market opportunities, globalization of its marketing and service capabilities is a top priority. In fact, for some Chinese firms, such as Lenovo, Haier, and TCL, one of their key motives in globalization is to expand markets abroad and to establish sales channels, service systems, and brand awareness. Overseas mergers and acquisitions offer the fastest path for such companies to establish their sales and marketing presence in the key U.S. and European markets.

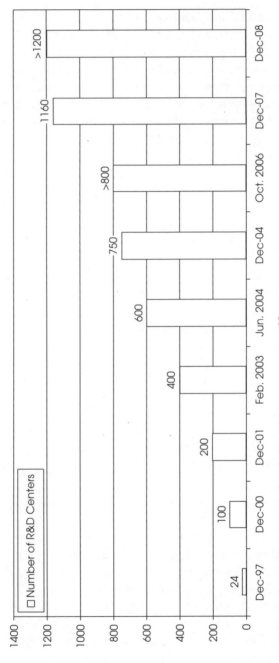

Figure 2.3 Number of Foreign R&D Centers in China[12]

Common Pitfalls of Globalization

According to Bain & Company's analysis of the performance of 7,500 listed companies in seven developed countries during the period 1996–2000, only one-sixth of those companies going global achieved sustained profit.[13] Therefore, companies should weigh the potential benefits of globalization with a realistic assessment of their capabilities. According to Leo Tolstoy: "All happy families resemble one another, each unhappy family is unhappy in its own way."[14] Although companies that have failed in their attempts to become global, each have their own stories; they share one thing in common—not having (or, indeed, knowing) the right objective. This lack can manifest itself in a number of ways, as the following examples illustrate.

A good example of this can be seen in the global expansion of Korean conglomerates, which ballooned without effective corporate management. By the end of 1998, Daewoo, the second-largest Korean conglomerate, which had inflated itself to 48 subsidiaries and 396 legal entities overseas, went bankrupt under the financial storm.

Japanese companies went on a "shopping spree" when the yen appreciated greatly after the Plaza Accord in 1985. Japanese companies made 45 acquisitions in 1990, the majority of which were luxuries irrelevant to their core business. Mitsubishi, for example, spent US$840 million to acquire a 51 percent shareholding in the Rockefeller Center, and Sony acquired Columbia Radio for US$3.45 billion. Japanese investment overseas amounted to US$400 billion from 1986 to 1991, which made Japan the largest direct investing country in the world. However, Columbia Radio caused Sony losses of US$2.7 billion, an amount that would have devastated a smaller company.

Companies that go global are generally well established domestically, but they tend to overestimate themselves and make rash decisions when going abroad. Deciding to enter the international market in 1986, Acer announced its ambition of "Realizing the Dragon's Dreams" and launched massive recruitment. It spent US$94 million to acquire Altos for its expertise in mini PCs. Unfortunately, shortly after the acquisition the industrial mainstream shifted away from mini PCs, resulting in record losses for the company in 1991. Its biggest mistake, however, was the acquisition of Service Intelligence. While the acquisition cost the company a mere US$500,000, the loss caused by poor management amounted to US$20 million. Acer founder Stan Shih reflected: "People tend to overestimate their abilities and opportunities. Managers should be aware of decision traps on account of human nature." BMW was another to learn a costly lesson from an ill-judged acquisition: its acquisition of Rover was to cost it US$3 billion. Though market expansion helps to spread risk and make new space for growth, it can also lead to diseconomies of scope. Professor C. K. Prahalad divides diversity into two categories:[15] diversity of businesses and diversity of national markets. Appropriate diversity creates value through strengthening corporate branding, skills and experience, and through the synergies created by different businesses. Yet it brings about more complexity and greater management costs, and diminishes corporate resources, especially the energy of the leadership. Diseconomies of scope happen when the cost exceeds what is created. What's more, diversity of markets means less investment in a single market. Companies should be sure that there are enough resources to support market expansion.

Incorrect forecasts and merely copying the domestic operation model can lead to failures overseas. For instance, supermarkets are popular in France but have failed in the Netherlands; in Germany, discount stores have more than 50 percent of market share but less than 10 percent in the U.K. and France. There are plenty of examples of failure among large retailers. Carrefour withdrew completely from the American market just five years after its entry in 1988. In Japan, the world's second-largest retailing market since 2000, it sold out to AEON in 2005 to end its short history in that country. Foreign markets, particularly Japanese markets, are hard to enter because it requires perseverance, promise, and uniqueness of products. BMW made a grand success in Japan because it realized that business there meant huge investment in trust and reputation from the very beginning. It actually made that investment as a selling point when entering the Japanese market in the 1980s.

Stages of Globalization

Globalization is an evolutionary process and Chinese companies have to learn to be patient. This gradual process will enable them to accumulate experience and reduce the level of risk inherent in entering unfamiliar markets. Professor S. T. Cavusgil[16] from the University of Michigan divided the internationalization process into five stages:

- domestic marketing
- pre-export stage, a preliminary analysis of international markets
- experimental involvement, small-scale export and trial-and-error international marketing
- active involvement, expanding investment in targeted key markets
- full-scale involvement, an international marketing strategy from a global perspective.

Chinese companies should heed such advice and deepen their involvement in the globalization process by accumulating experience and know-how through experimentation and learning. The approach adopted by Haier provides a good reference in this regard. As a leading domestic-appliance company in China, Haier mainly relied on exports to expand its international markets in the early stage. Then, starting in 1996, it set up factories in the Philippines, Indonesia, and Malaysia, because these were neighboring countries with a culture and economy similar to that of China. Eventually, it established a manufacturing base in South Carolina and became the first Chinese domestic-appliance company to open factories in the U.S. It also set up a marketing center in New York and a service center in Los Angeles to further expand its American market and use resources there to serve the group as a whole.

Notwithstanding its over-ambitious acquisition of the Thomson TV business in 2004, TCL, too, followed a similar path in the initial stages of expansion overseas. TCL launched color TV sets in 1993; 50 percent of this business was intended for export in 1994. During the Asian financial crisis of 1997–98, it established operations in Russia, Singapore, Vietnam, Indonesia, the Philippines, and India to build its presence, and acquired Donaco, a Vietnamese company, in 1998. After four years of endeavor, it had established itself among the top three in the Vietnamese market. In fact, while it was experiencing difficulties integrating with Thomson, its performance in emerging markets was substantial. Without the accumulation of experience and talent in those markets, TCL could have had a much more difficult time with its integration and acquisitions.

There are echoes too in Sony's experience. Though reliant on exports at the beginning, it then began to set up representative offices in New York, Hong Kong, and Zurich. It opened factories in Hong Kong and Ireland in 1959. The opening of a new branch in the U.S. signaled its entrance into the American market. The launch of ADR (American Depositary Receipt) in the U.S. in 1961 raised funds as well as brand awareness. In 1970, it became the first Japanese company to be listed in the U.S. and it opened its first U.S. factory in 1972. Over the following two years, it opened television factories in Spain and the U.K.

The Giant Group is one of the few Taiwanese companies that owns a global brand. It set up its European headquarters in the Netherlands in 1986, and American headquarters in 1987, a sales company in Japan in 1989, and sales companies in Canada and Australia in 1991. It entered mainland China's market in 1992 and opened factories in the Netherlands in 1996. With this step-by-step approach, it now has a sales network covering over 50 countries and regions. It is the leader in the global bicycle industry, with a 5 percent market share and revenues of US$1.83 billion in 2008.[17]

From these examples, it is evident that globalization cannot be realized by big leaps and bounds. Chinese companies must practice patience and be content with gradual evolution. It is by adhering to this philosophy that the likes of Huawei, ZTE, Haier, and Midea have become successful.

Global Ambitions

Japan and Korea rose from the ashes of World War II to enter Western markets, which makes their experiences and lessons worth learning from. With the launch of their economies, Japanese and Korean companies started to go global, most probably because they were faced with limited domestic markets and insufficient resources. But an entrepreneurial spirit accompanied by an international vision contributed to their expansion onto the global stage. Sony was a pioneer among Japanese companies, deriving its ambition from Akio Morita's visit to Philips in the Netherlands. Surprised to find that the electronics giant originated in a small town, he wrote home excitedly: "I'm exalted by what I saw here. We should be confident that our products can be well-received in international markets."[18]

Ambitions can arise from humiliation as well. When it was first established in 1969, Samsung was just a television supplier for

Sanyo. By the middle of the 1990s, it was still regarded as a low-end manufacturer, in spite of the fact that it had established an overseas manufacturing base in Portugal in 1982. During his market investigations in the U.S. in the early 1990s, CEO Lee Kun-Hee found that Japanese products were displayed in prominent spots and were being sold for premium prices, while Samsung's products were relegated to inferior spots and low prices. Indignant, he took 100 senior managers to the U.S. for another investigation and, in a dramatic display, burned Samsung products that were experiencing quality problems (including televisions, refrigerators, and mobiles) when he got back to Korea. Working under the slogan "Change everything except your wife and kids," Samsung is now a global company, deriving more than 80 percent of its sales from international markets. In 2002, Samsung's market capitalization surpassed Sony for the first time. By 2009, Samsung had become the largest technology company in the world, with annual revenues of US$117.8 billion.

Morita was by no means the only Asian entrepreneur to suffer humiliating experiences overseas. Zhang Ruimin, chairman of Haier, felt similarly humiliated during his first visit overseas in 1984 when one of his German friends told him that the most popular Chinese goods were fireworks. "I was hurt by this statement," he recalled. "Are we Chinese to live forever under the ancient four inventions?[19] I had a dream at the time that, one day, my products would sell in Germany and in global markets!"

In 1994, Huawei founder Ren Zhengfei made his company's ambitions very clear, saying: "The telecommunication equipment markets will be shared by three makers: Siemens, Alcatel, and Huawei." In 2008, Huawei registered the largest number of patents among all leading companies in the world. One year later, the company recorded revenues of US$21.9 billion, second only to Ericsson in the telecom-equipment industry.

From "Resource Advantage" to "Capability Advantage"

Although China's domestic market is large and growing fast, it is also highly competitive. Some international companies had established their operations in China long before the birth of many Chinese firms. Setting up factories in China gave them access to low-cost labor and high-consumer demand, which offset the national competitive advantages of Chinese firms. By confining themselves to the domestic market, Chinese companies will be merely painting themselves into a corner. Conditions today are very different from those which confronted Japanese and Korean companies in previous decades, when domestic markets were relatively closed, allowing them adequate time to build their organizational capabilities. However, Chinese firms are not as lucky, for globalization is now a must rather than an option. Acquiring resources, locating value-chain activities, and formulating competitive strategies must all be considered against a global backdrop, making globalization a necessary condition for survival to some extent.

Besides, Chinese firms are short in history, and weak in organizational capability, branding, technology, and innovation by comparison with their international competitors. Today, most Chinese firms have built their success on resource advantages, including low-cost labor, local and central government support, and preferential treatment. However, these advantages are being eroded by fierce price competition and the fact that international companies are transferring their manufacturing capabilities into China and rapidly squeezing the profit margins of Chinese companies.

As Lenovo has shown, Chinese firms have a strong entrepreneurial spirit, a sense of urgency, and an ability to adapt and survive in the face of fierce competition. However, Chinese firms, especially manufacturers, are facing bottlenecks in "soft strengths" rather than market space. Just as it was for Japanese and Korean products many years ago, the "Made in China" label bespeaks low-cost and low-quality to foreign consumers. The challenge to China is to transform its competitive edge based on resources and low-cost manufacturing into one based on technology and innovation, and to climb the "smiling curve" toward the two ends of the value chain. Globalization provides Chinese firms with strategic opportunities to restructure their competitive edge. Some companies have reinforced their competitiveness through global strategies, and have even developed new capabilities, while others have paid dearly for choosing inappropriate globalization strategies and paths.

The Japanese Model

In the early 1980s, the impact that Japanese companies were having in the United States led to considerable pessimism in American industry. Both industrial and academic communities devoted substantial attention to the review and analysis of the competitiveness of these two competing countries. The unique "Japanese Model of Management"—whose core concepts were the primacy of the customer, a focus on process rather than product, quality control across the organization, and an insistence on change and improvement— was what gave Japanese companies their cutting edge. Richard Pascale and Anthony Athos (1982) pointed out this competitive edge derived from management skills—vision in particular. Kenichi Ohmae (1991) emphasized that Japanese management was far more than company songs and lifelong employment. Most importantly, Japanese companies placed customers at the core of their strategy formulation and value creation. According to Michael E. Porter (2002), the Japanese company model was characterized by, among other things, high quality and low cost; a variety of products; lifelong employment which viewed employees as assets; consensus leadership with long-term objectives; and diversification to capture growth.

In addition to their competitive strengths in cost and quality, Japanese companies have been known for their commitment to globalization. Sony moved its headquarters from Tokyo to New York as early as 1963, with Akio Morita and his family making the same move. In a *Fortune* survey of American radio distributors in the 1960s, while most said that they had never distributed Japanese radios, they had distributed Sony radios—a clear indication that Americans viewed Sony as an American company. A survey report on global market leaders said: "There is no Japanese company—whatever size they are—that does not know what is going on with their largest competitors in the global market."[20] The global vision and ambition of Japanese companies are worth learning from.

If the Japanese Can, Why Can't We?

Chinese companies must realize that their current advantage in resources is not sustainable. As international companies transfer their production bases to China, competition for labor, land, and other resources will inevitably lead to rising costs of all kinds. The labor shortage in the Zhujiang Delta Region is a signal of things to come, and some firms from Zhujiang are to transfer their factories to countries where the cost is even lower, such as Vietnam. Besides, as the Chinese economy improves, there is increasing pressure from other economies for the appreciation of the RMB. Chinese firms that do not prepare for the coming changes will find themselves in trouble. Sony recognized long ago that it would have to adapt to changing circumstances: following the Plaza Accord in 1985, it began to transfer its production overseas and had established factories in Southeast Asia by 1990. Bharat, an Indian company, provides another example of the foresight necessary for survival. In 2005, its CEO was quoted as saying that: "No one can develop by counting on low-cost labor forever."[21] The company went on to invest US$55 million to update its equipment when its annual revenue was only US$0.12 billion. Thus, it made a foray into the international procurement chain and has now one of the best foundries in India.

Whether going global or not, Chinese companies are pondering over how to overcome their weaknesses and reinforce their competitive edge. They can do this by building capability to integrate global resources and by climbing the "smile curve" to core technologies, product innovation, branding, and sales. Many take globalization as a short-cut to improving their competitive capabilities and to narrow the gap with leading companies.

As shown in Figure 2.4, there are both push factors (for example, fierce domestic competition), and pull factors (such as new markets, technologies, management, and capital) at work in influencing Chinese companies to go global. The vice-president of Little Swan, Xu Yuan, said in a CEO Roundtable in 2007: "We must go abroad. The global demand for washing machines is 60 million, including 10 million in China. But China is only exporting two million out of our 30 million domestic production capacity."

A survey of shoe companies from Wenzhou city produces similar conclusions for the need to go global. These companies are mainly small or medium-sized enterprises (SMEs) and the biggest challenges they face are at the corporate level, in procuring appropriate talent and the need for effective branding. Competitors from the neighboring Fujian Province have managed to develop their own brands (brands such as Xtep, Anta, 361, and Erke shoes are recognized at home and abroad) and as a result were not as badly hit by the financial crisis as their peers without brands.

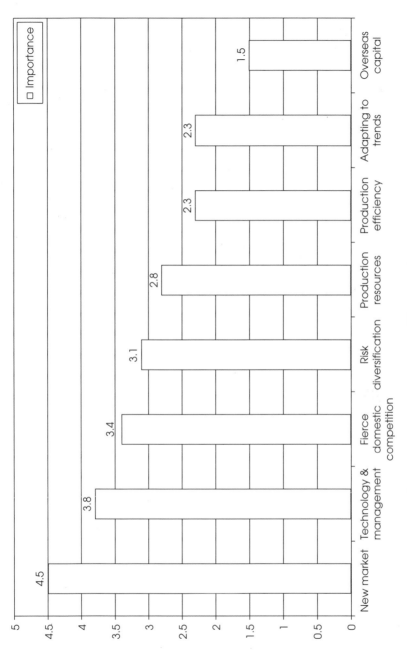

Figure 2.4 Motives for Chinese Firms Going Global[22]

□ Importance

New market 4.5
Technology & management 3.8
Fierce domestic competition 3.4
Risk diversification 3.1
Production resources 2.8
Production efficiency 2.3
Adapting to trends 2.3
Overseas capital 1.5

Beware of the Strategic Pitfall of the Japanese Model

After booming in the 1980s, Japanese companies slid into the "lost decade" of the 1990s. Professor Porter described this loss of national competitive advantage as a "collective loss of strategy." Originally, Japanese companies did the same thing as their competitors, only much better. This model enabled them to advance to the limit of business efficiency, eventually leading them to homogenous competition, and unreasonably low prices and profits. Japanese management was badly in need of a strategy to come to the rescue. No company can create a unique competitive edge through business efficiency alone, because best practices are distributed easily.

This conclusion may be enlightening to Chinese firms. Most Chinese companies are enthusiastic exponents of imitation and homogeneity rather than of innovation. Endless price wars lead to meager profits, which in turn causes shrinkage of expenditure in R&D, creating a vicious circle. Chinese companies should learn from their Japanese peers to shift from competition in price or quality to that of strategy and innovation.

The Paradox of "Chinese Price" and "Chinese Brand"

In 2005, a columnist for *The Christian Science Monitor* Sara Bongiorni[23] and her family conducted an experiment: They decided not to buy any "Made in China" products for one year. At the end of that year, Bongiorni concluded: "You can still live without it, but it's getting more painful and more expensive. A decade from now, I may not be brave enough to repeat such an experiment again." Though "Chinese price" is known to all and terrifies Western companies, global Chinese brands are unknown and certainly not feared (Nobel Prize laureate John Nash was quoted as saying: "We know Chinese products, but no Chinese brands"[24]). Take footwear as an example. The annual production value of the footwear industry in the Wenzhou region was RMB36.4 billion (US$4.4 billion) in 2004, with up to US$1.2 billion of this being exported. But, of the region's more than 3,000 shoemaking companies, there is not a single world-famous brand. China sends 20 percent of all its footwear exports into the EU, among which 60 percent are from Wenzhou.

Building a global brand will be the key mission of Chinese firms pursuing globalization. Acer from Taiwan has been there. Starting out as an original equipment manufacturing (OEM) company, Acer had been stranded by its lack of bargaining chips. Stan Shih lamented the fact that "MIT = 30% off."[25] In 1987, the company made the decision to give up its old brand, Multitech, and build the Acer brand, which had previously been shared by dozens of companies. J. T. Wang, current chairman of Acer Group recalled: "The brand is being built and destroyed at the same time, and the destroyers do not admit this truth." To address this problem, Acer introduced a "one brand" strategy. To ensure a clear and consistent brand value, other companies within the Pan-Acer group were not allowed to use this brand name. Brand has to be carefully guarded and nurtured as the Acer experience has shown.

Samsung stands out as an excellent example of an effective branding strategy. It made its presence known in the Interbrand Best Global Brands in 1999, ranking ninety-sixth. Since then it has gone on to overtake Sony (in 2005) and, in 2009, was ranked fifth.[26] After the Asian financial crisis, CEO Lee Kun-Hee asked the company to "promote the core strengths—the intangible asset and brand value—the source of competitiveness to the world standard" and regard the brand as "key driver of business growth." Knowing that top brands are based on excellent products, the company spared no effort in R&D. Samsung's R&D expenditure for 2005 was US$5.16 billion, 9.2 percent of its revenue, rivaling that of Intel. To build its brand image, Samsung invested up to US$4 billion in marketing annually. Moreover, since 2001 the company has terminated cooperation with mass retailers such as Wal-Mart—a move that took considerable courage and resolution—to sell its products exclusively in high-end retailers.

Know What You Want

It is especially important for Chinese firms to understand what their global weaknesses are. They also need to know what they want to gain from globalization. Considering their need for management know-how, assets, and clients, priorities have to be set. When talking about acquiring the PC business from IBM, Mary Ma, former CFO of Lenovo, said: "We argued a lot about whether we were able to manage or handle the joint-managing team on our own." Lenovo identified its objective: it wanted to purchase not only technology and assets, but also management skills. The latter became the key to Lenovo's successful integration.

Galanz, the global leader in microwave ovens, used strategic alliances to transfer the production lines of international companies to China. In this way, it purchased only what it needed without having the burden of human resources from overseas. When the Sheler Corporation was for sale, the Wanxiang Group from Zhejiang Province approached the LSB financial-services company with the intention of acquiring only Sheler's tangible assets. They finally reached an agreement for LSB to take over Sheler's employees and plants, while Wanxiang acquired the brand, patents, equipment, and markets, thus reducing the price from US$19.36 million to US$420,000.[27]

Obstacles to Overcome

In 2006, executive chief editor of *China Economics Quarterly*, Arthur Kroeber, observed that: "[In the 1970s] Japanese and Korean companies globalized from strength, but Chinese firms globalize from weakness." This continues to be true with regard to the current technology, talent, branding, and image of Chinese firms today.[28]

From 1997 to 1998, Little Swan, China's leading manufacturer of washing-machines, had its efforts to enter the Japanese market nullified by the Japanese Patent Association. To avoid lawsuits on patents, Little Swan entered into a strategic alliance with many international brands, including Panasonic, Meloni, NEC, Renesas Technology, and GE. As the industry leader in China, Little Swan now has a number of advanced key technologies in function design, technology R&D, and product development. Huawei is another Chinese company that emphasizes R&D and its proprietary patents enable it to avoid major legal challenges from competitors in the American market.

The current contribution of Chinese firms to the Western market is still that of providing low-cost imitations. Therefore, they face more challenges in merging and integrating with overseas companies. When Lenovo acquired IBM's PC business, *BusinessWeek* commented: "In essence, IBM outsourced its PC business to Lenovo, and Lenovo outsourced much of its management and sales to IBM."[29] Tong Haibin, associate general engineer of the Shanghai Machine

Tool Group, has admitted that Chinese companies have much to learn: "We are students learning global management. Our overseas employees can be our teachers in this topic. When going global, it is difficult for 'students' to lead 'teachers'."[30] This point was borne out in March 2005 when Korean executives from Ssangyong Motor reacted harshly when SAIC appointed five Chinese executives to Ssangyong: "Chinese executives lack experience in international business. They even have no experience to run an auto manufacturing company on their own. How can they convince our employees?"[31]

China's low-cost capabilities can also threaten employment in Western companies, a point acknowledged by K. Y. Lee, CEO of BenQ Corporation: "The term 'China' has great impact overseas, because it means speed and ability in cutting cost, implying restructuring of employment opportunities."[32] We can foresee that security of employment will be a key topic for negotiation when Chinese firms strive to acquire Western companies.

In recent years, the failure of some Chinese companies overseas is used as a pretext to "demonize" Chinese firms. Hence, companies wishing to go global must bear in mind that their problems can become the nation's problem. For example, when the Shougang Group acquired Hierro de Peru in 1993 for US$120 million, it promised to invest US$130 million in iron ore. Unfortunately, the effects of the Asian financial crisis meant that Shougang was unable to fulfill its promise and it had to pay a fine of US$25 million. Coincidentally, more than 170 accidents occurred in the ore mines in 2003 and intensified the local people's negative attitudes toward Chinese firms.

A lack of global management experience and skills is a fatal weakness of Chinese companies going global. An article in *German BusinessWeek* described how "Chinese firms are generally managed by a small group formed by several managers with unconditional loyalty to the leadership. The cohesion of a small group has advantages of making quick decisions, but often has shortcomings when analyzing the situation." Cross-cultural understanding is also a huge gap. The article continued: "After the acquisition of a German machine-tool factory, the Chinese company's director said at the town hall meeting: 'The Labor Union represents the employees' interest, but must also put the factory's interest first.'[33] After his speech, the employees stared at their new boss as if he was an alien."[34]

Summary

The ultimate goal of globalization is to create value. As we discussed, the national competitive advantage is the starting point of a company's consideration of globalization strategies. But, as the globalization of the economy progresses, the ability to integrate resources—rather than the resources themselves—is fundamental to a company's survival in the era of global competition.

To globalize successfully, companies must know why they are going global and what they want to achieve. Upgrading competitive capabilities is one of the motives for Chinese firms to pursue globalization but, in doing so, companies must have patience and persistence to go through the learning curve.

Entrepreneurs have to keep in mind that the only right objective of globalization is to create value, rather than to fulfill dreams for the nation. In acquisition negotiations, they must be ready to let go even at the very last minute. By pursuing the dream to become a "Top 500 company" many Chinese firms have ended up with losses. Globalization should not be a trap.

Globalization is never easy. Acer weathered the ups and downs to become what it is today. Samsung became a global brand by insisting on putting 8 percent of its revenue in R&D to pull itself through the Asian financial crisis. In short, it requires clear vision and big commitment to become a truly global firm.

Endnotes

1. Jonathan Birchall, "Wal-Mart to Push 1,000 Chinese Suppliers to Adopt Green Agenda," *Financial Times*, April 7, 2008.
2. Jack Welch, "Bringing Back a Wary Workforce," *BusinessWeek*, July 7, 2009.
3. Michael Porter, *The Competitive Advantage of Nations* (Boston: 1990).
4. Trend Micro is a transnational information security-software company and was founded in California in 1988 by Chinese-American Steve Chang. In 2006, its revenues were over US$700 million. The company is listed on both the Tokyo Stock Exchange and NASDAQ and has branches in 30 countries and regions and over 3,000 employees.
5. Harry G. Johnson, "The Efficiency and Welfare Implications of the International Corporation" in *The International Corporation: A Symposium*, C. P. Kindleberger (ed.). (Cambridge, Massachusetts: MIT Press: 1970).
6. James A. Senn. CEO Interview, Global Management Challenge. Georgia State University, Atlanta, 1995.

7. See also Maximilian von Zedtwitz, *International R&D Strategies in Companies from Developing Countries— the Case of China* (UNCTAD, 2005).
8. Tan Dizhou, *Louis V. Gerstner on IBM* (Shanghai: Yuandong Publishing House, 2005).
9. Harry M. Markowitz, "Portfolio Selection," *The Journal of Finance*, March 1952.
10. "Volkswagen Says China Sales Up 12.5% in 2008," *China Daily*, January 27, 2009.
11. Annual Report 2008, Duerr AG Bietigheim-Bissingen, 2009.
12. Wang Min, "China Becomes a Top Choice of R&D Centers," *Markets*, January 19, 2009; Men Hua, "An Analysis of R&D Centers in China" at http://www.chinacir.com.cn/expert/2009727171365.shtml. Accessed August 27, 2009.
13. James Root and Josef Ming, "Making Foreign Moves Pay Off," Bain Brief January 12, 2005.
14. The first line from his novel *Anna Karenina*.
15. C. K. Prahalad and Yves L. Doz, *The Multinational Mission: Balancing Local Demands and Global Vision* (London: The Free Press, 1987).
16. S. T. Cavusgil and J. R. Nevin, "Conceptualizations of the Initial Involvement in International Marketing" in C. W. Lam and P. M. Dunn (eds), *Theoretical Developments in Marketing* (Chicago: American Marketing Association, 1980).
17. Quincy Liang, "Giant Hits Record Revenue, Profits, EPS in 2008" at http://cens.com/cens/html/en/news/news_inner_26919.html. Accessed August 27, 2009.
18. "Sony and the People," Social Environmental Report, Sony Corporation 2002.
19. The four ancient inventions are paper, compass, gunpowder, and printing, as demonstrated in the Beijing Olympic Games Opening Ceremony.
20. Hermann Simon, *Hidden Champions: Lessons from 500 of the World's Best Unknown Companies* (Xinhua Publisher, 2000).
21. B. N. Kalyani, Chairman & Managing Director, Bharat Forge at the Business Standards Awards 2005 in New Delhi, March 24, 2005.
22. IBM Institute for Business Value/Fudan University, *"Going Global: Practices, Challenges, and Solutions"*, 2006.
23. Sara Bongiorni, *A Year Without "Made in China": One Family's True Life Adventure in the Global Economy* (Wiley Publishing Company, 2007).
24. Terill, 2004.
25. MIT refers to "Made in Taiwan."
26. http://www.interbrand.com/best_global_brands.aspx?langid=1000. Accessed August 2009.
27. Liu Xuemei, "Indian Rivals Challenge Wanxiang's Takeover Bid," *China Business* Feature, July 2006.
28. Statement during the 2006 Conference at the Kellogg School of Business at Indiana University about "Capitalism with Chinese Characteristics."
29. Steve Hamm, "Lenovo and IBM: East Meets West, Big-Time," *BusinessWeek*, May 9, 2005.
30. IBM Institute, 2005 op. cit.

31. Ibid.
32. Interview with K. Y. Lee on ChannelWeb, September 27, 2003.
33. In China, there are no labor unions in the Western sense. China's labor union is part of the government system and has no direct responsibilities in negotiating key work arrangements, salaries or work conditions.
34. *German BusinessWeek*, "Going to Germany," October 19, 2006.

3

The Strategic Choices: Think Before You Jump

It is not the strongest of the species that survives, nor the most intelligent. It's the one that's most adaptable to change.

Charles Darwin

Having a globalized economy entails the growth of market territories or the expansion of the hinterland from which resources are acquired; but it also has a profound effect on the nature of the competitive environment in which companies operate. Companies must change their competitive strategies accordingly or risk becoming the "dinosaurs of globalization."[1] If they desire to survive in an increasingly flattened world, they must create strategies for globalization, construct and modify their value chains, and make trade-offs with corresponding strategies. Only those with a global mindset will survive the unprecedented challenges that globalization presents.

Profound Change

Capabilities, not resources

The presence of abundant cheap labor makes "the Chinese price" unmatched globally and as enviable as the remarkable number of software developers in India. However, it does not mean that these resources are only available to China and India. Many multinational corporations have succeeded in moving their factories to China and outsourced their software operations to India to reduce their costs. Resources are no longer the exclusive property of their country of origin. The capability of firms to integrate resources around the world to create customer value is more important than the endowment of resources in specific countries.

Scale is more important

Galanz, based in the Guangdong Province of China, accounts for more than half of the world's output of microwave ovens.[2] More than 55 percent of the world's containers are produced by China International Marine Containers. The economies of scale enabled by such vast production create competitive strongholds.

Business is more focused

The direct impact of globalization is the exponential growth of both the quantity and quality of competitors, which requires companies to focus more on their core competence in order to survive. Evidence of this can be seen in the expansion of business process outsourcing (BPO), especially in the areas of logistics, procurement, engineering, marketing, sales, administration, and the legal, financial and accounting fields. In 1999, BPO in India was valued at around US$100–200 million. Since then, it has grown rapidly—to US$3 billion in 2006 and to about US$5.7 billion in 2008. Wipro Technologies provides offshore IT and BPO, and its income grew from US$545 million in 1999 to US$1.8 billion in 2005 and US$5.7 billion in 2009. It is currently the largest third-party provider of R&D services ranging from product strategy to software design and quality management. Currently, Fortune's top 500 companies have established 400 business centers in India or outsourced to Indian companies.

The rise of Taiwanese companies conforms to a large extent with the global trend of a deepening division of labor. In the 1980s, Morris Chang revealed a contradiction in the semiconductor industry—the key in chip design is talent and technology, but the main resource in chip manufacturing is capital.[3] Therefore, it is not economical for a company to be engaged in both chip design and manufacturing. To Chang's design, the Taiwan Semiconductor Manufacturing Company (TSMC) underwent a fundamental change in its strategic positioning such that it specialized in chip manu-facturing for chip-design companies, and never competed with its customers in the market. TSMC became the world's first chip manufacturer that did not design chips on its own, a move acknowl-edged by *BusinessWeek* as having "changed the rules in the semicon-ductor industry."[4] Similarly, the major reason that Advanced Micro Devices (AMD) was able to close the gap with Intel is that AMD let TSMC produce its chips while Intel was still engaged in both design and manufacture.

Specialization also means that large companies will outsource more parts and concentrate on their core components and technol-ogies. This provides more opportunities for Chinese companies that are known for being good manufacturers. Situated in Shenzhen, Acoustic Technologies Corporation (AAC) holds 40 percent of the contracts for the world's cell-phone speaker production. In 2008, AAC achieved sales of RMB2,256 million (US$324 million), and gross margin of more than 40 percent. Since 2004, after AAC estab-lished its solid position in the market for micro-acoustic devices, it expanded into other consumer electronics, including MP3 players, game consoles, notebook computers, and car alarms. It also became a producer for Dell, Compaq, Siemens, Nintendo, and other inter-nationally renowned companies.

Another Chinese company which has proved adept at gearing its production to the needs of the global market is the Fuyao Glass Industry Group Co. Ltd. Fuyao Glass was founded in 1987 and has become one of the top suppliers for all core segments of the world's glass markets. Starting in the vehicle glass-replacement market, it became the largest supplier to Toyota and also delivers to the luxury car-maker Bentley. Fuyao Glass exports have doubled since 2006. For 2009, expected revenues were predicted to exceed RMB5.4 billion (US$790 million), with more than 30 percent of this coming from overseas markets, where it is competing strongly with the two dominant players: Sain Gobain from France and PPG from the United States.

In a report about the trends that influence the global business environment, McKinsey has pointed out that globalization will bring about profound change in the ecosystem of companies.[5] In the future, three types of firms—which the report characterizes as "whales," "cuckoos," and "worms"—will cooperate to achieve mutual success. The "whales" referred to are the global giants such as Wal-Mart (which alone has more than 1.7 million employees). Cuckoos never build nests or feed their young themselves; instead, they lay eggs in the nests of other birds. As the functional departments of other companies, "cuckoo"-type companies form coexistent relationships with other companies and achieve continuous integration of the value chain. UPS, for example, delivers more than 60 types of logistic services to countless customers from 175 countries. The third type, "worms," are relatively small and highly adaptable companies. They aim at the niche market that large companies disdain to pursue, or provide services that other companies need but lack the funding to employ the specialists required for such work. Into this category would come accounting or consulting firms, or arbitrage experts, such as the institutional investors of pension funds. Like worms, small and ordinary creatures that do their work inconspicuously, these types of companies are productive in a surprising way.

A great example of a "worm" company is Nine Dragon Paper from Guangdong, the world's largest cardboard manufacturer. The company's product range includes container boards, liner boards, duplex boards, and pulp. After entering the Hong Kong Stock Exchange, the "Dragon Lady" Zhang Yin has become one of the richest business women in China. Her fortune is said to be based on imported scrap paper from North America and Europe, but she considers herself not as the "queen of wastepaper", but would rather be known as "queen of container board." Her thinking exemplifies the focused business model of the company: collecting waste paper and turning it into packaging materials. Large portions of these container boards are used for exporting Chinese goods to the rest of the world. The company's rigorous focus on the needs of the transportation industry shaped its organization and process. Having a focused market approach and the vision of large demand in this market has enabled the Dragon Lady to outpace large global competitors in this competitive market.

The Essence of Strategy

For today's Chinese firms, "strategy" has become a platitude. However, very few Chinese firms have been able to grasp the essence of strategy. There are only rare cases where companies stand out for their excellent business strategies. Professor Michael Porter, the guru of business strategy, pointed out that the essence of strategy resides in activities—choosing to perform activities differently or to perform different activities than rivals, and to create trade-off effects in competition.[6] Southwest Airlines, based in Houston Texas, is a classic case of formulating and executing this type of strategy. This airline provides only short-distance, low-cost, point-to-point services between medium-sized cities and metropolitan areas rather than the traditional spoke-hub model with connecting flights. The efforts of other airlines to imitate Southwest Airlines have been in vain, because they were unable to give up their original positioning. We see here that the essence of strategy is the trade-off of investing a company's limited capital in high-profit growth opportunities.

China has its own success story in the airline industry: Hainan Airlines, the fourth-largest in China, is a privately owned airline that is less than 10 years old. The company succeeded in a government-controlled environment, where routes, prices, and airline expansion are strictly regulated. Hainan Airlines changed the conventional idea that flight services are confined to on-board services alone by introducing the concept of "flight products" in China. It is the first Chinese air company to pass ISO9000 quality certification, and has grown into an important company with great potential. The company intends to continuously re-invent itself in order to become the top airline of choice for passengers in China and around the world.

Globalization Strategy

Globalization strategies also require companies to have clear trade-offs, re-positioning them to take advantage of market opportunities and critical resources around the world, creating more competitive differentiation and advantages. Globalization is two-pronged, incorporating both market opportunities and resources. For the former, companies may choose to compete in the domestic market or in global markets. Equally, they can leverage resources domestically or globally. On this basis, we can divide companies into four business types based on their strategic focus (see Figure 3.1).

Figure 3.1   The Strategic Focus of Globalization

The global resourcer

These types of companies use resources globally to enhance their competitiveness in the domestic market, and to equip themselves to compete more effectively against both domestic and foreign firms. For instance, Ctrip and China Life Insurance use foreign capital through overseas listing. Alibaba obtained search-engine technology through its acquisition of Yahoo! China, thereby utilizing foreign technologies to enhance its operations in China. Li Ning, the Chinese sporting-goods company, hires European, American, and Japanese designers to take advantage of global talent to develop the domestic market. SAIC and other Chinese firms bring in foreign technologies and brand resources through joint ventures. As latecomers to global competition, Chinese firms must be adept in utilizing global resources if they are to catch up and outstrip the competition.

Situated in Guangzhou, the Pearl River Piano Group is an excellent example of growing into a world champion by utilizing global resources. Today, the company produces almost 100,000 pianos annually, which accounts for 70 percent of its domestic market, while its market share in the U.S., Germany, and other mature markets is 30 percent. In the 1980s, Pearl River Piano Company hired Bud Corey, the production manager of the established brand Wurlitzer, as a consultant to supervise all manufacturing processes. Over a period of some 10 years, Corey brought the company the core technology of piano manufacturing. The company also invited a number of top designers from Europe and America and paid them huge sums (as much as RMB20,000 (US$2,410) per day, compared to the average Chinese annual income of RMB10,000 (US$1,205) for their expertise and advice. At their recommendation, the company brought in equipment from Germany, Japan, South Korea, Italy, and the United States. It was a huge investment but one that undoubtedly paid off.

Guangdong's Galanz Group has proved itself to be very capable of utilizing and integrating global resources. Utilizing its accumulated retained earnings, it purchased the most advanced production equipment from Toshiba and persuaded companies in France, Japan, and South Korea to transfer microwave production lines and configuration devices to China. This enabled these companies to focus on branding and marketing activities while Galanz offered ODM services to them. As a result, Galanz was able to increase the number of production lines from one in 1993 to 20 in 2002, thereby reaping significant advantages from economies of scale.

During its growth phase, the Neusoft Corporation, a software and outsourcing conglomerate, focused on alliances with multinational companies in order to learn from and absorb the management know-how of its partners. It works closely with Toshiba, Hitachi, Sony, Oracle, and more than 20 other renowned companies as its partners. In June 2004, it established a joint venture with Philips Electronics— Neusoft Philips Medical Equipment System Ltd. It also formed a partnership with EMC of America, and started localization of EMC software. Through such cooperative ventures, Neusoft has enhanced its overall R&D, production, and international marketing capabilities and established itself as a brand with international recognition.

The global exporter

This type of firm takes advantage of abundant and inexpensive endowments of labor, land, raw materials or other resources in its home country to produce and then sell products around the world. Such firms typically produce domestically and sell globally (including both home and overseas markets). Companies such as CIMC, the Midea Group, and Changhong Electric are classic examples of global exporters. In China, global exporters are concentrated primarily in the manufacturing industry (rather than the service industry, as is the case in India), as this best reflects China's cost advantage at this stage.

However, there are certain limitations for global exporters. The very competitive TV industry is a good example of such limitations. In the past, numerous television companies competing for the global market lowered their prices repeatedly only to find that other countries eventually invoked anti-dumping measures against them. In October 1994, for example, the European Union levied anti-dumping duties of 28.8 percent on all color TVs exported by Chinese companies. In December 1998, this was increased to 44.6 percent, a measure that was revived again in March 2006. In 2008, the World Trade Organization (WTO) filed 34 anti-dumping cases against Chinese companies, ranging from circular welding pipe to alloy steel castings.[7] Although Chinese companies have attempted to circumvent these measures in various ways (TCL's acquisition of the German Schneider and French Thomson TV manufacturing units, for example), China's steel, automobile glass, agricultural products, clothing, and many other industries have also suffered from anti-dumping laws.

Global exporters could also be disadvantaged by their lack of foreign sales channels. The Chinese TV giant Sichuan Changhong was eager to enter the U.S. market. However, deceived by the financial fraud of its U.S. distributor, APEX, it lost up to US$470 million. All these are heavy prices to pay when global exporters need to count on overseas partners to sell and promote their products.

A new type of global exporter has emerged recently. Such businesses are built around foreign-educated Chinese entrepreneurs, who bring to bear industry and technology knowledge acquired in foreign markets, along with overseas customers. By understanding the changing needs of the global market and applying Chinese cost advantages, global exporters can now be found in some of the high-tech industries.

Verisilicon Inc., founded by Wayne Weiqiang Dai, is such an example. At the height of the Internet boom, Wayne Dai quit his tenured professorship in computer engineering at the University of California at Santa Cruz and set up Verisilicon in China to provide customized technology products and services. Under his guidance, Verisilicon established the biggest chip-design library in China. The company's business model was based on technology innovation, but delivered only chip-design service, which was its founder's specialist area. Dai also hired the right people—experienced chip designers from Silicon Valley, Taiwan, Japan, Korea, Nice, Beijing, and

Shanghai. Through combining the most advanced technology and the cost and human-resource advantages available in China, the company now boasts the likes of Fujitsu, NEC, TSMC, and Bosch among a client base numbering more than 500. The company has some 240 engineers, 30 of whom are based in the United States. Its primary operation is in Shanghai, with other design, operation and support offices in Silicon Valley, Dallas, Tokyo, Nice, Taipei, and Seoul. Customers in the U.S., Europe, and Japan account for half of its revenue, while the other half comes mostly from mainland China and Taiwan. The company generates the bulk of its income from intellectual-property licensing fees and royalties. The remainder comes through microchip design and turnkey services that develop initial specifications into packaged and tested chips for a wide range of industries that include automotive, machinery, toys, voice-control audio, and wireless communications (2G-3G, voice-over IP, WiMax).

Another example of a thriving Chinese company built around the expertise of an overseas-trained founder is Wuxi Pharma Tech, one of the world's leading target-drug R&D outsourcing services. Li Ge, its founder, earned both master's and doctoral degrees in organic chemistry from Columbia University, where he co-invented a technology used for new drug discovery. He was also one of the founding scientists of Pharmacopeia Inc., a NASDAQ-listed bio-pharmaceutical company. With this expertise, Wuxi Pharma Tech outgrew many of its peers and hired more chemists in 2009 than traditional companies like Pfizer. The company employs more than 2,500 full-time scientists and in 2008 recorded sales revenues of US$261 million. It provides both lab facilities and scientists to established pharmaceutical companies around the world, which serves to both reduce expenses for U.S. and European drug-makers, and opens up opportunities for young Chinese scientists. The company has also acquired a U.S. chemistry-services company, App Tech Inc., to expand its overseas activities.

Other companies to mention in this regard are Suntech Power Inc., the world's largest producer of crystalline silicon-photovoltaic (PV) modules; Rene Sola Ltd., a leading global manufacturer of solar wafers; Jetion Holding Ltd., a manufacturer of solar cells and solar modules; and Beijing 1000 Science Technology Co. Ltd., the leading-online learning platform for English in China.

The global player

This type of company utilizes global resources to compete for global markets, making full use of advantageous local resources to build its international competitiveness. Such companies (which include Trend Micro, TCL, BenQ, Lenovo, and Haier as mentioned earlier) are the most difficult to manage and have the most complex type of global positioning.

Hong Kong's Li & Fung Group is an excellent example of a company integrating global resources to compete globally. Founded in 1906, the Li & Fung Group initially only engaged in traditional trading. With the liberalization of the economy, manufacturers were becoming much less reliant on trading companies, and in 1995 Li & Fung realized that its future was at risk if it did not take timely steps to address the matter. Over the next few years, the company acquired its biggest competitors, greatly expanding its customer base in the United States and Europe and bringing in more talent and customer resources in the process. Through acquisition and introducing diversity in marketing, Li & Fung has transformed itself into a leader in the international supply-chain management business. Its global network covers more than 40 countries and regions. It hires 24,000 employees, has suppliers from 5,700 producers in 42 countries, with exports amounting to US$8.5 billion—an achievement grounded in its ability to integrate global resources to create value for its customers.

Hon Hai Precision Industry Company Ltd., better known in mainland China as Foxconn, is the foremost provider of joint-design, joint-development, manufacturing and assembly services to global computer, communications, and consumer-electronics companies. The Foxconn Group is the largest and fastest-growing multinational manufacturing-services provider in the world. Originating in Taiwan, it employs more than 550,000 people (450,000 in mainland China) and has revenues of US$52 billion. Founded by Terry Gou in 1974, the company has expertise in providing the lowest-cost solutions in mechanical and electronic parts. Foxconn is a typical "original design manufacturer," producing parts for the likes of Apple (iPods, iPhones, Mac mini . . .), Dell, Hewlett Packard, Sony (PlayStation), Nintendo (Wii), Microsoft (X-box), Motorola (cell phones), and Amazon (Kindle). Its focus is truly global. Outside China, it manufactures in the Czech Republic, Hungary, Mexico, Brazil, India, and Vietnam, and has sales offices in Europe, North America, Latin

America, Southeast Asia, and Australia. The only thing Foxconn does not have is a brand, which means that the general consumer does not know what a great global company it is.

The local player

While this type of firm competes solely in the domestic market with domestic resources, it is nevertheless involved in globalization, albeit passively, when foreign competitors enter the domestic market. Such is the case for numerous food and beverage companies, retail and department stores and supermarkets, whose domestic bases are now under challenge from foreign competition. Companies may choose to remain solely in the domestic market because they lack the overall strength to support a move into oversea markets, the nature of the industry in which they operate makes such a move difficult, or the rapid growth of the domestic market provides enough room for future development.

It must be stressed that the strategic focus of globalization is dynamic. Firms can adopt different strategies at different stages according to the changes in their capabilities and comparative advantages. BenQ, for example, started out purely as a local player, and was primarily engaged in manufacturing peripheral IT products for the local Taiwanese market. In the early 1990s, the company began to set up factories in Malaysia, Mexico, and China to take advantage of cheap foreign labor, and thus became a global resourcer and, eventually, a global exporter. Creating its own BenQ brand, it rapidly set up more than 30 sales branches in Europe and the U.S. Later, when it acquired the Siemens cell-phone business, it increased the number of sales branches to more than 70, and became a real global player.

So, how can firms choose the right combination of markets and resources, and identify the focus of globalization strategies in line with their own capabilities?

The Key Questions of Globalization

We believe that the focus of a firm's globalization strategy should be made in full consideration of the following four issues:

- What are the company's target markets?
- What resources does it have or not have?

- What are its core competencies and strengths?
- How prepared is its global talent pool?

Target market

In considering whether it should explore international markets, it is not sufficient for a company to take this route simply because its domestic competitors have done so. Whether a firm should enter a foreign market depends on the speed and room for growth in the domestic market. If the domestic market is already saturated, it may be time to consider going global. For instance, in 2000 Lenovo had become the leader in the Chinese domestic PC market, with a more than 30 percent share. To increase this further would have required considerable effort. Therefore, to benefit from economies of scale and to reduce costs, it had to expand its market abroad. In cases such as this, going global becomes a natural choice. In contrast, for companies like Alibaba, Lianhua Supermarket, Pacific Insurance, and Vanke Real Estate Limited, the room for domestic development is still very large. The better choice for them is to focus on their domestic market to take advantage of their familiarity with their respective market situations and their established business networks. Southwest Airlines, Telefónica Telecommunications of Spain, and Lloyd's Bank of Britain, for example, focus primarily on their domestic markets, with remarkable results. Decisions to go global should be considered, rational, and based on market conditions, rather than simply following what others are doing.

In addition, the extent to which the firm's products or service offerings can be standardized across different markets is another key consideration. The greater the degree of standardization possible, the smaller the business risk and the easier it is for economies of scale to come into effect. For example, given the nature of the business in which it operates a, company such as Trend Micro, which produces anti-virus software, is only relevant operating across many countries. The majority of household electrical appliances, communications, and computer products also belong in this global category. On the other hand, for industries such as real-estate development, accounting, insurance, financial services, or telecommunications, whose products or services cannot be standardized across national boundaries because of economic, cultural, and regulatory differences, it will be more difficult to go global. Overseas markets are not a homogeneous whole. Developed countries and developing countries offer entirely different opportunities and challenges. While penetrating into the markets of developed countries provides enormous opportunities and excitement to challenge and compete with world-class players in the most critical markets, the challenges are enormous as it requires relatively strong brands, advanced technologies and high-quality products to succeed and survive. Sophisticated organizational capability is needed to be a player in that arena. If a company decides to pursue such a path, it has to find an appropriate market entry point. Though Haier is relatively sophisticated in management know-how amongst firms in China (see also Chapter 8), it entered the U.S. market with great caution. In fact, it gradually expanded its brand influence by targeting niche market segments, rather than competing head-on with General Electric, Whirlpool, and other international giants.

In contrast, markets in developing countries are more similar to those in China and companies might be well advised to choose these markets as a starting point and training ground for them to work on and reduce the difficulties and risks involved in moving overseas. With some experience behind them, they would then be better equipped to face the bigger challenges presented in developed countries. This is the strategy of "capturing the cities by surrounding rural areas" as articulated by Mao Zedong. Through years of operation in Southeast Asia, South America, Northern Europe and Africa, Haier finally expanded successfully into the North American mainstream market. In the 60s, Honda of Japan entered the U.S. motorcycle market, only to find out that the market for high-powered motorcycles was tightly controlled by Harley-Davidson and other local companies. Honda therefore turned to the neglected lightweight motorcycles; with prices only one-fifth of ordinary motorcycles, they became highly popular, elevating Honda to global leadership by the 1970s, with a U.S. market share of 80 percent. By being cautious at the outset, avoiding the mainstream U.S. auto market and concentrating on motorcycles and small cars, by 2004 it had established for itself a 10 percent share of the overall U.S. auto market.

Resources

Globalization opens up new possibilities for companies to acquire better and/or cheaper resources,[8] and provides opportunities to realign activities along the various value chains. Firms should assess what resources they currently have and what resources they need to achieve future growth and then decide whether these should be obtained domestically or globally. When a firm finds that resources within the country are not adequate to meet its strategic needs (including insufficient quantities of capital, energy, oil, minerals, and cheap labor, or insufficient quality in talent, technology, and brand awareness), it must ponder how to leverage foreign resources.

The primary aim in resource utilization is to make the best use of the comparative advantages in resources of different regions. There are two major types of resource utilization based on the principle of comparative advantage. The first is to shift non-critical business activities to low-cost countries, thereby allowing the company to run high value-added and core business in its own country. For instance, although many Western multinational corporations possess cutting-edge technologies and well-established brands, they are faced with high labor costs at home. To enhance their competitiveness, they need to reduce their costs significantly and thus transfer their production bases to, say, China or India. The other type of resource utilization is to acquire superior overseas resources to make up for shortages at home. Although there are huge business opportunities in mainland China, many Chinese companies encounter financial shortages because the financial markets there are still in their infancy. However, through listing overseas or through receiving venture-capital funds or private-equity funds from overseas companies, Chinese firms can gain access to the financial resources they need and, at the same time, improve their corporate governance. Baidu (China's largest Internet search engine, with revenues of US$184.7 million in 2009), Ctrip (a one-stop China travel service) and Bosideng (which produces half of China's branded winter coats, with revenues of more than US$626 million in 2009) are among the many Chinese companies which have used foreign capital successfully.

For Chinese firms, the supply of abundant and inexpensive labor is an obvious advantage. However, most of them lack resources in areas such as capital, technology, branding, and human resources with the appropriate training and experience. Such resource gaps are even more obvious for those firms that benchmark themselves against world-class companies and aspire to compete in the global market. For this reason, the five companies which took part in our research project all consider globalization as a good opportunity to acquire overseas resources that are in critical shortage.

CIMC, for example, built up its economic scale by acquiring more than 10 domestic competitors but still lacked its own core technologies. To address this problem, the company acquired some overseas companies and a large number of patents, which gave it critical technologies related to the production of cold-storage containers and foldable containers (see Appendix 2).

TCL, Lenovo, and BenQ were all successful in China, but to become world-class, they had to overcome their gaps in talent, technology, brand recognition, and overseas channels. They were able to gain the resources they needed by acquiring business units from multinational companies or by setting up R&D centers in the U.S., which gave them access to the superior technologies, talent, and information there. However, it should be noted that although Chinese firms face similar problems in this regard, conditions within each will vary and business leaders will need to assess their own situation and decide accordingly, rather than simply follow what other companies are doing.

Core competencies and strengths

Only when a company has a clear idea of its own strengths and weaknesses in comparison with other global market players can it make reasonable trade-offs and decide on market positioning. To proceed without this information is likely to do more harm than good. When considering the strategic focus of globalization, a firm's core competence will largely influence two critical decisions: what kind of overseas markets to enter (developed countries vs. developing countries) and what business approach to use to penetrate such overseas markets (through own brand or OEM).

As discussed earlier, many Chinese companies lack brand recognition in developed European and North American markets, where the "Made in China" label still carries negative connotations. It is much less difficult, however, to enter developing markets in Asia, Latin America, and Africa, where the business environments are quite similar to China and local rivals are relatively weak. Consumers there, whose priority is more likely to be price than quality, accept Chinese goods more readily. As Chinese firms still lack core competencies, it is wise to choose these developing countries as breakthrough points. The experience of the likes of Huawei, ZTE, and other telecom-equipment producers shows the benefits of adopting such an approach.

As for the developed markets, it is risky to enter them recklessly. Excellent Chinese brands would still be viewed as a synonym for poor-quality goods in the U.S. and European markets, and it would take a long time to gain customer recognition. The Taiwan Giant Global Group is one of the few firms that possess globally renowned bicycle brands. It entered the U.S. market in 1987, but it did not manage to break even until 1999. Similarly, Huawei's breakthrough into the U.S and European markets is attributable to its long-term accumulated technical strength. Huawei now has the largest number of patents among Chinese firms; its cumulative number of registered patents has reached 10,000. It owns more than 3,000 patents in the 3G field, and 5 percent of basic patents on WCDMA, making it fifth in the world.

Having a clear understanding of its core competencies enables a company to identify its business approach in going global. Identifying its core competence as lying in manufacturing, rather than in global brands or channels, Galanz was able to succeed in overseas markets by offering low-cost manufacturing capabilities to multinational companies.

The availability of global talent

When considering whether or not to enter the overseas market or use overseas resources, a company should also take its global talent pool into account, something that is often neglected. As Acer's founder Stan Shih pointed out: "Globalization can't be rushed. To build the capability in globalization, talent is the top priority."[9]

Competing in the global market is a test of a company's organizational capabilities. The original business knowledge and strategy applied in the domestic market may not be transferable overseas. Only global talent can help businesses to adapt, replicate, or create new capabilities to compete in new overseas markets. For example, some managers of Chinese firms may have excellent sales experience in China, but may prove to be ineffective in an unfamiliar new market. Similarly, merger and acquisition capabilities in the domestic market cannot be simply replicated in overseas markets. At this point, only personnel who are familiar with business operations in those overseas markets can help the company establish itself abroad. It is very dangerous for companies to be overly confident about their success and experiences in home markets and underestimate the importance of having people with knowledge and experience of market conditions overseas. When a company lacks such talent, it should use a more cautious, step-by-step approach to develop overseas markets and/or utilize global resources.

Although some of the necessary global talent can be obtained through external recruitment, a company can still face problems of cultural and company assimilation. Therefore, it is fundamental that senior business leaders have a global mindset and cross-cultural leadership skills. The fact that Trend Micro has become a successful global player is not only attributable to its founders' extensive experience of studying and working abroad, it is also due to the fact that its core leadership team of 13 members has been drawn from six countries and very diverse cultural backgrounds.

While many Chinese firms currently lack this expertise and experience, they can begin to overcome this obstacle by upgrading and developing their talent base at home by acquiring talent from multinational firms, learning more advanced management systems from established global corporations, and competing with world-class companies in the domestic market. This was exactly the focus of sporting-goods company Li Ning's globalization strategy prior to 2008. By competing with Nike and Adidas in China, it developed and enhanced its talent and systems in various aspects of business operation, ranging from product design and brand marketing, to supply-chain management.

Second, companies can also purposely and systematically develop such talent in their early stage of globalization. For instance, companies such as TCL, Huawei, and others were able to develop the necessary talent base in the early stage of their respective globalization processes by sending employees to open up developing-country markets in Eastern Europe, Asia, Africa, and other regions. By doing so, they not only explored the global markets, but also developed their global talent pool gradually.

Another option open to companies which have an obvious talent gap is to borrow talent for short-term support. This is what Lenovo did when it gave the CEO and other leadership positions to Steve Ward and his IBM team. While some members of the media criticized Lenovo for outsourcing its management,[10] this move reflected the pragmatic approach adopted by Lenovo in admitting that its own leadership team was then not up to par and bought it time to develop its own talent.

Globalization Strategy Requires Candid Self-knowledge

While the two dimensions of "market focus" and "resource utilization" can help firms clarify the strategic focus of their globalization strategy, the ultimate choice of their strategic focus must be consistent with their core competencies, organizational capabilities, and availability of global talent. To gain an objective understanding of one's real strengths and limitations is no easy task; companies need to be both realistic and patient. In the face of criticism and ridicule, Galanz adhered to its concept of providing "global factories" for others. Although Huawei has developed a number of the best products in the world, and possesses a sophisticated management system, it does not set up factories overseas, nor does it engage in expansion or acquisitions hastily. Lenovo is an even better example of facing reality. It takes candid self-understanding to allow more internationally experienced talent from IBM and Dell to fill its top management positions.

Indeed, globalization is more a journey than a destination. Based on a clear assessment of current circumstances and conditions, companies need to think ahead and build up their global capabilities proactively rather than waiting to react when opportunity knocks on the door. Chinese firms could learn from the experience of India's Bharat Casting. Recognizing that it could not continue to grow by relying on low-cost labor alone, the company invested US$55 million on upgrading technology and equipment, even when its annual sales were only US$120 million. This enabled it to become a procurement supplier for multinational companies and it is now one of India's most successful casting firms. To be successful in the rising tide of globalization, firms must abandon short-term thinking, and have a long-term vision for the future.

Hidden Champions

If a company has powerful R&D and market-development capabilities, it is reasonable for it to compete head-on with multinational corporations. However, when facing the reality of a relatively short organizational history and weak organizational capability, it would be more rational for the majority of Chinese companies to avoid areas dominated by multinational corporations and, rather, to focus on niche markets.

The opportunities for specialization enabled by globalization make "hidden champions" possible. The so-called hidden champions are companies that hold strong competitive positions in certain areas but are largely unknown. They are hidden because the nature of their products is B2B, or their products escape notice in the end products (for example, no one pays much attention to the label on a beverage bottle), or they deliberately avoid the radar of the media. In general, these firms are utilizing Porter's niche strategy, but on a global scale. Because they concentrate their energies in one niche market and command a high market share, usually much higher than their biggest competitors, these companies may not be widely known to the public (see Table 3.1). Union Knopf, the world's largest button manufacturer, produces 250,000 kinds of buttons. Approaches such as these are encapsulated in the company philosophy of BBA, a British textile company: "Our tactic is to dominate our market niches by transforming the general market in which we are nobody into market niches where we are somebody!"[11]

Shanghai Zhenhua Port Machinery Co. is an excellent example of targeting a niche market and silently growing into a world champion. The company was founded as recently as 1992, but by 1998 had become the leader in the container-machinery industry, with a world market share of 25 percent. The respected British magazine *Cargo Systems* reported that in 2005 Zhenhua had increased its world market share to 70 percent, 20 times that of its nearest rivals. Zhenhua's products are installed in more than 90 ports in 54 countries and

Table 3.1   The average market share of Hidden Champions[12]

Market	Absolute market share	Market share of biggest competitor	Multiple of relative market shares of hidden champions
World	30.2%	19.4%	1.56
Europe	36.7%	20.8%	1.76
Germany	44.4%	21.8%	2.04

regions, including Taiwan and Hong Kong. How did yesterday's "nobody" defeat the giants?

Situated on Changxing Island in the Yangtze River Delta Region, Zhenhua has built the world's largest and most technically advanced large-scale production base, covering an area of about a million square meters. Having access to abundant labor resources enables Zhenhua to submit tenders that that are considerably cheaper than those of its competitors. However, the company realizes that it cannot maintain its position as an industry leader by relying on low cost alone. It therefore invests more than 5 percent of its sales revenue on R&D, an investment which has paid off: to date, Zhenhua owns more than 30 patented new container-machinery products, which are all in leading positions in the industry. To ensure timely delivery of equipment to its customers, Zhenhua also owns 13 carriers (most of its competitors do not offer transportation services) and is involved in transporting 70 percent of the world's port machinery. Even after attaining dominance in its niche market, the company's founder, Tongxian Guan, insists that he will stay focused on the company's strategy. "My strength is in the steel structure," he said; "I will not set foot in industries where I do not have advantages."[13] The company's ambition is to sustain its current role while simultaneously developing machinery for related heavy-marine and cargo-handling industries. Its vision is to form a complete value-chain in this industry.

Founded in 1959, Hong Kong's Johnson Electric is the world's largest independent motor manufacturer, producing more than three million motors every day. Its products are used in cars and a wide range of consumer-electronics products. The company has 39,000 employees and sub-contractors in 20 countries. In 2009, its sales amounted to US$1.74 billion.[14] A focus on products and the tremendous advantages derived from economic scale also ensure that the company maintains a leading position in R&D and product innovation.

The Beijing Vimicro Corporation, founded in 1999, is another Chinese company which has been able to compete in a computer-chip industry dominated by U.S. and South Korean firms. Through focusing on digital multimedia chips as a starting point, it now has a 60 percent share of the world's image-input chip market. Now, at least six out of every 10 digital cameras worldwide utilize Vimicro's "Xingguang" digital multimedia chips.

Summary

The powerful forces of globalization have changed many aspects of competitiveness, making capability rather than resources a key to success. It has also raised the required scale to be globally competitive and deepened the regional specialization of many companies around the world. Attempting to compete without a strategy is akin to a blind man riding a blind horse: it is impossible to reach a goal when it cannot be seen. Globalization does not mean that all firms should expand or that they should do this as quickly as possible. When participating in global competition, firms should give full and careful consideration to their organizational capabilities, choose the right target markets to focus on, and/or integrate cheaper or better resources to reach the next level of competitiveness. Different strategic focuses make different demands on a firm's organizational capabilities and global leadership skills. For latecomers in today's globalized economy, choosing to be hidden champions could be a wise option to start with.

Endnotes

1. Stephen H. Dunphy, "A WTO Anniversary Worth Noting: Economic Memo," *Seattle Times*, December 3, 2000.
2. According to its own press releases from August 2, 2008.
3. Tung An-chi: "Taiwan's Semiconductor Industry: What the State Did and Did Not Do," *Review of Development Economics* 5, December 2002: 266–88.
4. "China and the WTO: Will its Entry Unleash New Prosperity or Further Stabilize the World Economy?" *BusinessWeek*, October 22, 2001.
5. *How Companies Act on Global Trends: A Mckinsey Global Survey*, April 2008.
6. Michael E. Porter, "What is Strategy?" *Harvard Business Review*, December 1996; and Michael E. Porter, *Competitive Advantage* (New York: Free Press, 1985).
7. *WTO News*, April 28, 2008.
8. As mentioned above, the strategic focus of globalization is to continuously adjust and evolve. Lenovo's strategic focus in the 80s was to utilize overseas resources, but turned to becoming a global player in the 90s. In fact, in the early stage of their globalization, firms such as Galanz, CIMC, and BenQ were all global resource users before they became global exporters or global players.
9. Todd Crowell, "Winners and Losers," *Asia Week*, February 18, 2000. See also Stan Shih, "Me-Too Is Not My Style," The Acer Corporation, no publication data.
10. Hermann Simon, *Hidden Champions of the Twenty-First Century: The Success Strategies of Unknown World Market Leaders* (Springer, 2009).

11. Ibid.
12. Ibid. "The multiple of the relative market shares of hidden champions" is the ratio of the hidden champions' absolute market share to that of their biggest competitors.
13. Haiqiang Li, "The Dream of the Port Machinery Empire," *Global Entrepreneur* 123, June 2006.
14. Refers to fiscal year ended March 31, 2010.

CHAPTER

4

All Roads Lead to Rome: Paths to Globalization

Enter through the narrow gate. For wide is the gate and broad is the road that leads to destruction, and many enter through it. But small is the gate and narrow the road that leads to life and only a few find it.

St. Matthew 7:13–14

Once a company has clarified its strategic focus for globalization, the next step is to identify the appropriate paths to arrive at its destination. In recent years, the wide publicity given to Chinese firms pursuing cross-border mergers and acquisitions (M&A) has often misled people to believe that M&A is the only means to go global. In fact, not only is this a false perception, it is also a dangerous one. So what are the possible paths to go global? How should a firm choose the most suitable path?

Choosing a Path

When considering the path to pursue, companies must consider the following alternatives: Should the company go global on its own or through collaboration with overseas firms? If the company decides to go on its own, should it do this through internal organic growth, external mergers and acquisitions, or strategic alliances?

Table 4.1   Strategic focus and path selection[1]

Pace of Market Entry	Market Expansion	Resource Acquisition
Incremental Approach	67%	30%
Leapfrog Approach	33%	70%
Total	100%	100%

Each of these paths has its pros and cons. Organic growth may be slow but the company can control the rhythm and risks, giving it enough time to gradually learn and build global capabilities. Mergers and acquisitions are fast but integration is difficult and the failure rate is high, especially for cross-cultural integrations. Strategic alliances can help the company enter an overseas market quickly, but the relationships between partners are often unstable and uncontrollable.

The choice of path can be different at different stages of the process. Depending on its strategic aspirations and organizational capabilities, a company can choose different paths (or a combination of paths) at different stages, as we saw in our earlier example with the BenQ Group. The path a company selects is closely related to its strategic focus. Research shows that firms focusing on expanding overseas markets are more likely to prefer an incremental approach; that is, organic growth. On the other hand, companies focusing on acquiring overseas resources are more likely to adopt M&A and other leapfrog approaches (see Table 4.1).

Organic Growth

Organic growth is the gradual accumulation of globalization capabilities and resources achieved by the expansion of the company's existing businesses. For example, during the process of expanding into the global market, Haier developed its market country by country, including building factories and distribution channels in the U.S., completely through organic growth. Trend Micro, Huawei, and ZTE all adopted this path. Huawei waited for more than three years in Russia before its first order came. Organic growth means going forward one step at a time; it is a slow process, but it is the mainstream path for globalization. Its benefits come gradually, which allows time for learning and gives the company the opportunity to enhance its organizational capabilities in a gradual and controllable manner. Furthermore, organic growth can better ensure the consistency of the firm's managerial system and culture, unlike the sudden new culture brought in by acquisition.

Haier's decision to set up a factory in the U.S. gave rise to a great deal of doubt. *The Wall Street Journal* commented at the time: "A Chinese appliance maker has placed its bet on a counter-intuitive strategy."[2] Zhang Ruimin, chairman of the Haier Group, explained, "Calculating only the labor cost of setting up a factory in the U.S. has already violated the globalization concept. More importantly, we should consider the total cost [of entering the U.S. market]."[3]

However, organic growth has obvious limitations, as Chen Qiyu, vice-president of Fosun Pharmaceutical Corporation, acknowledged: "The first barrier for us to enter the European and American market is getting accreditations. Even if we had the accreditations, it would be a very long journey and would take tremendous efforts for local consumers to accept a Chinese brand. Indian firms faced the same problem when entering the European and American markets."[4] Leading Chinese firms such as Lenovo and TCL have opted for organic growth, but facing major bottlenecks on technology, brand recognition, and other areas, they turn to overseas M&A.

Mergers and Acquisitions

M&A refers to gaining rapid global expansion through the acquisition of overseas firms. As we saw in earlier chapters, TCL, Lenovo, and BenQ have all made acquisitions that have enabled them to become world-class players in their fields. There are also considerable synergies to be gained through cross-border M&A (see Figure 4.1). Generally, these come from either cost reduction or income from innovation. The former is less difficult, and takes less time to realize.

However, acquisition is a double-edged sword. The risk is high, and the rate of successful integration is low. When the failure rate of cross-border acquisitions is higher than the divorce rate of Hollywood stars, it would be very naive indeed to hope that one's company will be one of the lucky ones. Research shows that 61 percent of the world's cross-border acquisitions end up in

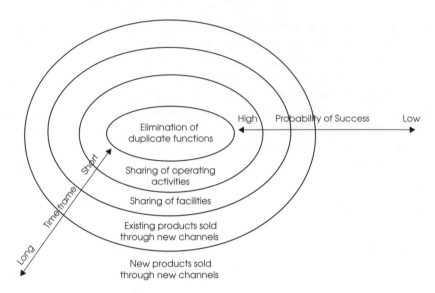

Figure 4.1   Map of Synergies[5]

failure.[6] Firms must realize that the risk is not limited solely to the acquisition price; it can be much more. BMW acquired Rover for £800 million (US$1,228 million) in 1994. When Rover was sold six years later, BMW reported a net loss of £3 billion (US$4.66 billion). Similarly, Acer acquired the U.S. firm Service Intelligence for US$0.5 million, but lost US$20 million on the project. In the same way, BenQ would have faced collapse if it had not ceased its investment in its handset division, which brought the BenQ-Siemens subsidiary into bankruptcy in 2006. Stan Shih, founder of Acer and a director of BenQ, once advised: "Never fight a battle that you can't afford to lose."[7] This is good advice, which any company seeking to go global would be well advised to heed.

To avoid bitter failure resulting from impulsive action, CEOs should also bear in mind the words of Kellogg CEO Carlos Gutierrez: "Although this is our dream deal, I tell myself abandoning it is no big deal."[8]

A further warning regarding the potential traps that can come with acquisition was given by Luo Yiqiang, a former member of Philips Global Management Board, who said: "You must think clearly about what you are buying. If we are only buying the brand, we should understand that it is the previous organizational capabilities that built the brand. Once you have bought the brand, it will depreciate over time."[9]

Strategic Alliances

Strategic alliance refers to collaborating with other (in this case, overseas) firms with complementary skills/needs to form one interest group. C. K. Prahalad and Y. L. Doz have repeatedly stated that the formation of strategic alliances is often the result of different intentions, such as treating the partner as a temporary arrangement and a springboard for long-term competition, saving resources, or merely the means to adjust short-run competitiveness.[10] OEM, joint ventures and resource exchanges are the most common forms of strategic alliance.

Philips and Sony's experience in the joint development of the CD player is a classic case of a successful international strategic alliance. In the 1960s and 70s, Philips developed the basic CD-player technology but, realizing that it would face competition on the standard from the likes of Telefunken, JVC and Sony, agreed to pursue a joint development with Sony, whose system was most similar to its own. By the end of 1981, more than 30 companies had signed licensing contracts with Philips-Sony, and Telefunken and JVC eventually withdrew from the competition.

Other renowned joint ventures include Samsung and Sony, and LG and Philips in the production of LCD panels for televisions. Similarly, in January 2006, four domestic color-TV giants, TCL, Skyworth, Konka, and Changhong, joined forces with Shenzhen Shenchao Science and Technology Investment Co., Ltd. to establish Shenzhen Julong Optical-Electronic Co., Ltd., to launch a sixth-generation TFT-LCD panel production line. They were joined in this venture by the BOE Technology Group, which injected RMB8 million (US$1 million) for a 40 percent stake in Julong Optical. These companies realized that they would have to combine their resources if they were to have any chance of challenging the Japanese, Korean, and Taiwanese dominance of this industry.

Under the multiple constraints of technology, brand recognition, distribution channels, and other factors, OEM is a rational choice for many looking to join the global competition. Acer, along with the vast majority of Taiwanese firms, adopted OEM as the first stage of its engagement in international operations. Having started out in low-profit assembly production, Acer then acquired first-class technology and manufacturing techniques through cooperation with multinational corporations, which eventually helped it rise continuously toward the two end points of Stan Shih's "smiling curve" (see Chapter 1). While expanding its production of motherboards, peripheral equipment, and other upstream products, Acer also developed new channels, built independent brands, and gradually freed itself from the role of a processing and assembly agent.

The world's top four sports brands—Nike, Adidas, Reebok, and New Balance—give their orders to Taiwan's Pou Chen Group. In 2009 shoe production of Yue Yuen, the group's shoe production subsidiary, reached 246.2 million pairs, securing a global market share of over 20 percent and sales of US$5.02 billion. Galanz's cooperation with more than 250 multinational corporations is a typical case of how productive strategic alliances can be. The Aokang Group has also adopted this model, forming a strategic alliance with Italy's leading shoemaking company Geox. Under this arrangement, the Aokang Group is in charge of Geox's production, sales and network-building activities in the Chinese market, while using Geox's global sales network to sell its own products in the overseas market. Geox has made the Aokang Industrial Park for International Brands its only Asian production base, and Aokang its sole global partner. While adhering to its organic growth-oriented strategy, Huawei Technologies also uses strategic alliances to enhance its competitiveness. Huawei has cooperated with Texas Instruments, Motorola, Intel, Microsoft, AT&T, Sun and other multinational giants on technology and marketing, and has set up joint laboratories. The establishment of Huawei-3Com is another attempt by Huawei to work with multinational companies in order to develop international markets.

The Haier Group attaches great importance to its strategic alliances in its growth process, having laid the initial foundations for its technical expertise through its joint-venture· production with the German company Liebherr. In April 2004, the Hisense Group announced its cooperation with Flextronics, a Fortune 500 company in the U.S., and invested in a Hungarian factory that produced a million color-TV sets annually. This arrangement gave Hisense indirect entry into the European market and enabled it to avoid the EU quota restrictions.

The Jiangsu-based Geoby Group had been a market leader in baby-strollers since 1996, but found it hard to penetrate the markets of developed countries until it forged an alliance with the Dorel Juvenile Group in the U.S. Under this arrangement, Geoby sells its strollers under Dorel's list of brands. The arrangement allows Geoby to both produce and design baby-strollers. Today, the Geoby

Group is the world's largest manufacturer of baby-strollers. Its sales income reached nearly RMB5 billion (US$760 million) in 2009, and captured 70 percent of the Chinese market, 50 percent of the Japanese market, and 40 percent of the U.S. market.

In 2005, Wenzhou's Chint Electric Co., Ltd. established a joint venture with GE, which has proved to be mutually beneficial, giving GE access to the mainland China market and Chint access to world-class technologies and management standards.

For weaker firms, a strategic alliance provides excellent learning opportunities depending on their desire to learn, their willingness to accept what is learnt, and the degree of transparency between the partners.[11]

Merely having a strategic alliance is no guarantee of international success, however, as Michael E. Porter has pointed out.[12] To maintain strategic alliances, there has to be mutual trust and, more importantly, mutual economic benefits. It is as well, too, not to become over-reliant on one party and companies must work to protect their own interests. The consequences of not doing so can be damaging. For example, in 2004, Bird, China's second-largest mobile-phone producer, entered a strategic partnership with Siemens under which Bird would open its nationwide network of 30,000 retail outlets for Siemens mobile products in exchange for technological support and a €5 million (US$6 million) investment to build distribution channels and retail shops. Unexpectedly, in June 2005, Siemens announced the sale of its mobile-phone business to BenQ, and the Bird–Siemens love affair came to an abrupt end.

Another example worth noting in this regard is that of AMD, which was once an authorized manufacturer of Intel products. Having worked in collaboration with Intel for more than 15 years, AMD suddenly launched its own AMD386CPU, and began to challenge Intel's market dominance. By 2008, AMD had grabbed 19.2 percent of global market share.[13]

Strategic Focus Influences Choice of Path

Apart from the considerations of risk, speed, and control, the choice of path toward globalization also depends on the company's strategic focus and its ability to function and manage as an international organization. Only with clear goals can companies choose the right path.

If the firm's strategic focus is to acquire overseas resources, M&A is a common approach. For instance, CIMC obtained key technologies and patents through strategic acquisitions (see Appendix 3). Firms can also bring in international technologies through strategic alliances, as Haier did in the 1980s when it made use of Liebherr's refrigerator technology to develop its own kingdom of white goods. But if global resource users mainly intend to utilize the cheap labor available overseas, they often adopt the organic growth path, setting up overseas factories or buying abroad.

As mentioned earlier, strategic alliances can work well as an entry point into international markets for companies that lack experience in overseas sales, brand recognition or resources. For example, Galanz could have chosen to create its own path into the competitive world of microwave ovens, knowing that it would not only have had to invest heavily in its areas of weaknesses (brand and distribution channel), but would also have had to fight against powerful multinational corporations. It chose, instead, the path of cooperation with more than 250 world companies, as their OEM manufacturer. In this way, Galanz ingeniously circumvented the trade barriers and secured market share beyond that of its own brand (see Appendix 6).

Global Capability Determines the Path

Global capabilities refer to the managerial abilities to integrate, coordinate, and fully utilize global resources and business opportunities. At the core of organizational capabilities are people, which make it especially important to know how to use and manage talented individuals from different countries and cultures in following the company's vision. Companies should help managers and employees around the world make the right decision and do the right thing in their own positions. This requires that companies have globalized values and mindsets, a management team competent in multinational business operations, and organizational design and operating systems capable of working on a global level.

Apart from possessing the necessary global operational capabilities, the company should also have a management system and methods that are compatible with and convincing to the merged party. Otherwise, cross-border confusion and internal friction could ensue and allow competitors to snatch the company's valuable customers and personnel. CIMC is an example of how M&A can be used successfully. When CIMC acquires another container company, it promptly merges that company's procurement and distribution systems into its own system, which quickly creates synergies. Thus, while CIMC's manufacturing is decentralized, the manufacturing systems of its subsidiary companies are still closely connected.

While globalization brings fresh challenges to internal R&D, manufacturing, supply-chain management, marketing, channels, and other aspects of business, the greatest advantage of organic growth is that it provides adequate time for a firm to gradually enhance its organizational capability. Moreover, it also makes it easier to maintain consistency in internal corporate culture and management systems, as the examples of Trend Micro and Acer clearly illustrate.

Relatively speaking, strategic alliances make the lowest demands on a firm's global capability, because the firm need only send a small number of managers to negotiate and cooperate with its foreign partners. Our study found that a capacity for cross-cultural management and an ability to integrate resources are the most important factors in determining the choice of approach toward globalization.

Cross-cultural management ability

An inevitable requirement of globalization is the ability to manage organizations across different cultures. Whether a company chooses to develop through cross-border acquisitions, organic growth, or strategic alliances, wherever cultural differences exist, there will be management challenges in the areas of communicating with personnel from different cultural backgrounds; in establishing mutual trust and respect; in overcoming cultural differences; and in balancing local requirements with the need for global consistency.

The most basic requirement of cross-cultural management is the mastering of the language of communication and the understanding of other cultures. Therefore, it is not hard to understand why Lenovo's Yang Yuanqing and TCL Thomson's Zhao Zhongyao worked so hard to learn English and understand the European and American cultures. However, a deeper problem is the potential for clashes in approach to communications, for example. Research has shown that Chinese firms tend to be flexible and informal in their approach to communication and collaboration, while Western companies are very particular about the systems and processes. Another potential problem arises from different perceptions of the relationship between employee and company. Chinese firms generally view voluntary overtime work as natural, and may even demand that key employees are contactable at all times. These requirements are almost unimaginable to Western employees, whose responsibilities to the company are based on the terms of a clear contract signed in advance and whose attitudes to incentive schemes may be quite different from those of their Chinese counterparts. It takes clear communication, a willingness to learn and adapt, and a great deal of patience to win respect and recognition from the management and staff of companies which have been subject to acquisition.

Cross-cultural management capacity is a "soft" skill for which practice is essential if cultural conflict caused by internal friction is to be avoided. Establishing joint ventures with foreign partners is a good way of acquiring experience in this regard. During the process, the Chinese side must negotiate with foreign managers, and make joint decisions, which helps in the mutual accumulation of cultural understanding and adaptability.

The key to cross-cultural management is to have management personnel who have had experience of working in other countries, and this is precisely what many Chinese firms lack when it comes to controlling large-scale cross-border M&A. TCL's Li Dongsheng, for example, found a serious shortage of personnel with the overseas experience necessary to undertake this role. "Even though we were aware of the work needed for the European operation," he said: "The limited amount of resources we had at that time forced us to let the European division operate in its original mode for quite some time after the merger."[14] As a result, the European operation incurred huge losses, and eventually led to reorganization and retreat.

Acer's Stan Shih believes that a clash of cultures was the main factor contributing to the failure of BenQ's acquisition of Siemens' mobile-phone business.

Resource integration

The strength of a company's ability to deploy and integrate its resources globally[15] is another determinant of the path it will select. Different paths have different requirements in this regard.

For mergers and acquisitions, for example, the ability to integrate resources is indispensable if the anticipated cost, supply-chain, and distribution synergies are to be realized. The key to GE's success in its aggressive acquisitions is that it owns a set of resource-integration systems and processes built on organizational experience. Mexico's CEMEX Inc. has grown into the world's largest producer of ready-mix concrete through a unique approach to cross-border acquisitions. Chinese companies currently lack both experience in cross-border M&A and effective knowledge-management systems. They are too heavily dependent on people rather than systems.

In addition, integrating resources reveals the differences and gaps between different countries. For example, TCL discovered the high cost of layoffs in Europe only after it had acquired Alcatel's mobile-phone business. BenQ's unsuccessful acquisition of the Siemens mobile-phone division has also been partially attributed to its insufficient grasp of the extent of Siemens' original losses and the rapid decline in its competitiveness, which caused the project to be delayed and resulted in an inability to reduce costs.

Establishing and maintaining strategic alliances also presents challenges to a company's ability to integrate its resources. A strategic alliance is essentially a complex game in which, as the experience of Galanz has shown, the key is to use one's own advantage in a particular area, and identify the complementary area of the partner, thereby establishing a common interest group, and continuously communicate and coordinate to ensure both parties fulfill their respective responsibilities.

For a company which takes the path of organic growth, its success is dependent on how effectively it uses its resources around the world to set up R&D, financing, production, marketing, and other bases, and how it integrates its global resources through key processes, information systems, and centralized authorization to achieve synergies in areas such as global procurement, international financing and credit, foreign-exchange management, product development, and manufacturing. As we saw earlier with the example of Trend Micro, the key to all of this lies in global management systems and making the best use of the human resources available in different parts of the world for specific tasks.

Because organic growth enables companies to follow their own rhythms in taking advantage of the global resources, it is the most controllable and presents the least difficulty in integrating global resources.

Self-knowledge

It should be clear by now that companies must have a clear under-standing of their motives and capabilities if they are to choose the correct path to globalization. There are, however, attitudes/beliefs on the part of Chinese firms that could cloud their vision and hinder their success. For one, opportunistic tendencies tempt some firms to go abroad without a clear idea as to why they are doing so or how to go about it. The overestimation of capabilities based on purely domestic success leads inevitably to disappointing results. Jim Hemerling, David Michael, and Holger Michaelis (2006) point out that, at the strategic level, many Chinese companies are unclear about their role and lack portfolio-management experience in different markets. They do not have a deep understanding of the consumers, competitors, channel structures, and regulatory environment in the markets they are targeting. In addition, their internal governance systems are also far behind those of large international corporations. At the operational level, Chinese companies do not yet possess the measures for effective selection, evaluation, and post-merger integration of their acquisition targets, making it difficult to achieve the potential synergies brought by M&A. Another major obstacle for Chinese companies lies in cultural differences. Western companies and Chinese companies operate very differently. Chinese firms tend to be entrepreneurial and their corporate culture is characterized by a strong patriarchal system and an emphasis on personal loyalty. At the same time, their decision-making and management processes are rather disordered. To realize integration of such a culture with the "professionalism" emphasized by the majority of Western firms, there has to be extraordinary sensitivity, determination, and flexibility.[16]

For example, after acquiring Siemens' mobile-phone business, BenQ not only failed to achieve its stated aim of "completing 10 years' work in two years," but also reported a loss of €840 million (US$997 million) in less than a year, and a drop in global market share from 4.8 percent to 3.2 percent. Eventually, it had to amputate the Siemens branch to survive. The failure resulted from a lack of ability to integrate and run the acquired business effectively. Among the 15-person BenQ–Siemens management team, there were only two members from BenQ: the chairman and the chief financial officer; the CEO position continued to be held by a German. The problem was that the German team was slow to respond to consumer trends, and, because the chosen design departed from the trend, the first dual-brand model released performed far below BenQ's expected standards. The slow response to market trends proved to be a fatal weakness, making losses inevitable. In the process of integrating with Siemens, BenQ showed a lack of experience and self-confidence.

A study by Accenture summarized the unique obstacles and opportunities of Chinese firms going global at operational, human capital, and macro politico-economic levels (see Table 4.2). Though Chinese firms have a good foundation from which to launch their global aspirations, the obstacles are also huge, requiring significant time and investment if they are to be overcome.

Table 4.2   Assessment of organizational capabilities for Chinese firms going global[17]

	Particular problems Chinese companies face when going global	Factors working in their favor
Operational	•Chinese companies going global have to come to terms with very different management styles, cultures, priorities, and mindsets.	•With a higher labor-to-capital mix, Chinese companies are more flexible in adapting processes than their Western counterparts.
	•They also have to conform to international standards, systems, and processes. Their corporate-governance framework, in particular, remains underdeveloped.	•Chinese companies have the advantages of local knowledge and cultural overlap in Asia's fast-growing markets that are the main target of today's multinationals.
	•Chinese companies have so far struggled to establish international brands. No Chinese companies have been featured in the *BusinessWeek*–Interbrand 100 Top Global Brands.	•Chinese firms still enjoy a significant cost advantage over Western multinationals, which tend to set up only selected operations in China.
Human Capital	•Chinese companies often lack managerial expertise and experience.	•There is a strategic push to nurture new talent in science and technology in China. There were about 5.59 million college graduates in 2008.

(Continued)

Table 4.2   (Continued)

	Particular problems Chinese companies face when going global	Factors working in their favor
	•Chinese companies still face obstacles in the competition for talent. Non-Chinese multinationals still enjoy advantages in pay and prestige.	•The bi-cultural Chinese talent—Western-educated and familiar with Chinese culture and values—provides a valuable resource for Chinese companies going global.
Economic and Political	•The recent outcry surrounding Chinese purchases abroad, particularly in the United States and the European Union, has highlighted protectionist obstacles to China's globalization.	•The prospect of further currency revaluations will reduce the cost of overseas acquisitions for Chinese companies.
	•State influence on corporate planning may lead to the pursuit of goals beyond profit maximization.	•China's "national champions" receive cheap land and finance, tax breaks, and preferential access to listing their shares.
	•Large state firms in protected industries are likely to be less efficient due to the lack of competitive pressures.	•By operating in previously protected markets, large state-owned firms have accumulated cash that they can use to buy assets abroad.

The Know-how of Overseas Acquisition

While overseas acquisitions can be exciting, they can also be painful experiences, as Acer, BenQ, TCL, Lenovo, and many others can all testify. Our research shows that acquisitions that are low-profile and progressive are more likely to achieve success. In contrast, greedy and aggressive jumps often end up in failure. Nevertheless, the restructuring and transformation of multinational corporations triggered by economic globalization creates excellent opportunities for firms from developing countries to acquire high-quality assets.

According to Citigroup, from 2006 to 2008, U.S. and European companies sold assets worth US$50 billion to Asia, with Taiwan, mainland China, and South Korea being the main buyers.[18]

These included YFC-BonEagle Technology's acquisition of the U.S. firm Prime and Wireless; and the Thunder Tiger Group's acquisition of Associated Electrics Inc., which enabled it to become the third-largest brand of remote-control models.

The mainland's Wanxiang Group is another player with a strong record of cross-border acquisitions. In 1993, Wanxiang began its preparations to go global in Kentucky. In August 1997, it received an official order from General Motors, which made it the first Chinese automotive-parts supplier to a first-tier whole-car manufacturer in America. That same year, Wanxiang purchased 60 percent shares of the AS Company and established Wanxiang Europe Bearing Company. Over the years, it has acquired some of the oldest and most-respected auto-parts suppliers in the U.S., including Zeller, LT, UAI, and the century-old Rockford Powertrain Inc., the inventor and largest supplier of wing-type drive shafts. Currently, the Wanxiang Group owns more than 30 joint-venture companies and its overseas income has reached US$300 million. There are a few learning points that can be drawn from Wanxiang's successive wins in overseas M&A: (1) to reduce the risk of over-valuing the acquisition only acquire companies whose strengths and weaknesses you are familiar with from previous business dealings; (2) only acquire part of the shares in general, seeking common development with the original company, to reduce the difficulty of integration; (3) do not engage in large-scale acquisitions, even when failure would not result in too many losses.

Chinese companies must realize that the integration difficulties and management requirements of overseas acquisitions are totally different from those associated with domestic acquisitions. CIMC started off with a number of domestic acquisitions and was able to enforce its own rules entirely. However, when it chose to enter the U.S. semi-trailer field, its strategy was much more conservative because it was unfamiliar with the American market and lacked previous experience of cross-cultural integration. It was obliged to be cautious, adopting a step-by-step approach. As CIMC president Mai Boliang advised: "Go abroad in small steps but at a fast pace. Do not make big strides. That is too risky and we cannot afford to take the wrong step"[19]

Learn from the Masters

After analyzing hundreds of mergers in the 1990s, Phillip Zweig outlined the major causes of M&A failure as follows:[20] (1) inadequate due diligence by the acquirer or merger partner; (2) lack of compelling strategic rationale; (3) unrealistic expectations of possible synergies; (4) paying too much; (5) conflicting corporate cultures; (6) failure to quickly meld the two companies. Looking at recent overseas M&A activities by Chinese firms, the pertinence of Zweig's list is worthy of further reflection.

Although acquisition is considered highly difficult and highly risky, some companies have shown that it is indeed possible to make acquisition a powerful tool for business growth. So, how do these acquisition masters operate?

From 1993 to 2001, Cisco Systems acquired approximately 70 firms and pushed the company to become the leader in global networking equipment. There are two key points to Cisco's acquisition strategy: careful selection of targets, and efficient and reliable promotion of integration. In fact, the acquisition opportunities that Cisco has given up outnumber its actual acquisitions. The company asks the following questions to help it think rationally: Do both sides share a common vision? Can the acquisition create value for shareholders? Does the acquisition produce long-term benefit for relevant interest groups (employees, customers, shareholders, and so on)? Are the cultures of the two firms compatible? Cisco has a highly efficient and experienced integration team, which usually starts integration the second day after the M&A announcement. This enables it to retain the talent of the other party. In 2002, the staff turnover rate of Cisco's acquired companies was only 2.1 percent, far below the industrial average of 20 percent. Since 2001, Cisco has acquired another 50 companies and has reinforced its market dominance.

GE Capital became GE's money-making machine through a series of acquisitions, contributing more than 40 percent of GE's profit in 2007. Since the 1930s, the company has engaged in more than 1,000 acquisitions and possesses a well-established acquisition and integration system. The key component of this system is the integration manager. As GE's former CEO Jack Welch put it: "Getting the right integration leader constitutes 95 percent of the success of integration."[21] Inside GE, the position of integration manager is viewed as an important opportunity for personal development, and is the goal of many highly talented individuals. The company's integration teams have at their disposal a web-based knowledge-management system that enables any one of them to access the collective wisdom and know-how of GE on making integrations work.

Summary

Our research shows that globalization does not necessarily entail a physical going out. Companies can still reach out to the world without leaving their domestic base, as the example of Galanz shows. M&A is not the only choice of going global; organic growth also achieves respectable results. It should be noted that the choice of strategic focus and implementation path must be in accord with the firm's organizational capability, and companies must act accordingly. Presently, the most urgent task facing Chinese firms is to come up with the vision and the courage to improve their global organizational and management capabilities. Only in this way can they seize the opportunities ahead and strive to succeed.

Japanese and Korean corporations had more failures than victories in the early stages of their globalization. There are two lessons to be learned from them: First, understand why you are going abroad. These firms bought vast amounts of real estate overseas because the opportunity was there; this resulted in serious financial losses. Second, do not act beyond your capacity. Many big South Korean consortia made huge expansions in the international market, but did not possess the core competencies and foundations to support multinational operations. These firms were devastated in the financial crisis. Currently, Chinese firms are avoiding the first trap, but the second trap is not easy to avoid, as TCL Group president Li Dongsheng has pointed out:

> The strategic direction of globalization is not wrong. However, the pace and rhythm of globalization are crucial. The early research, evaluation, and preparation of the project are also very important. Although estimations have been made, it is difficult to predict all adverse circumstances. The difficulties estimated before have occurred almost without exception, while unexpected problems also arise. The synergy we expected is not achieved as quickly as expected. Therefore, estimate the difficulties of globalization more comprehensively, grasp the pace and rhythm of globalization better.[22]

The risks associated with cross-border operations and management are very high, but experienced firms can greatly reduce these risks with practice in the domestic market and gradual overseas expansions. Galanz is known as a "price butcher" in China. Its cost advantage has become an effective weapon in its negotiations with multinational companies. CIMC acquired more than 10 domestic competitors, and accumulated strong integration experience. The essence of the CIMC "running fast in small steps" philosophy is risk control, and not letting the risk exceed the limits. Huawei first chose the East European market as its breakthrough point. CIMC's first acquisition in the U.S. amounted to only US$4.5 million. These cases all reflect this principle.

Endnotes

1. Bent Petersen and Torben Pedersen, "Twenty Years After: Support and Critique of the Uppsala Internationalization Model," workshop paper for presentation at the 22nd Annual EIBA Conference in Stockholm, December 15–17, 1996.
2. Kelly K. Spors, "Against the Grain: A Chinese Appliance Maker Has Placed Its Bet on a Counterintuitive Strategy: It's Bringing Jobs to the U.S." *Wall Street Journal*. September 27, 2004.
3. Hu Yong, "Two Decades: Haier Lessons," *China Entrepreneur* 10, 2006.
4. During the SAPA-GP 2008 Annual Pharmaceutical Industry Conference: "A Look at the Present and the Future" Ambler, Pennsylvania, June 21, 2008.
5. G. Cullinan, Jean-Marc Le Roux, and Rolf-Magnus Weddigen, "When to Walk Away from a Deal," *Harvard Business Review*, April 2004.
6. Kate O'Sullivan, "Secrets of the M&A Masters: Revealing the Paths to a Successful Deal," *CFO Magazine*, September 1, 2005.
7. Li Bo and Zhang Liang, "Talking to Stan Shih," *Global Entrepreneur*, December 2004.
8. Kellogg Company CEO Carlos Gutierrez, during the 2002 negotiations on the US$3.9 billion acquisition of Keebler Inc.
9. Yiqiang Luo, during his lecture at Tsinghua SEM MBA program, July 2003.
10. Yves Doz and C. K. Prahalad, *The Multinational Mission: Balancing Local Demands and Global Vision* (Free Press, 1987).
11. See also C. K. Prahalad and Gary Hamel, "The Core Competence of the Corporation," *Harvard Business Review*, May–June 1990.
12. Michael Porter, *Competition in Global Industries* (Boston: Harvard Business School Press, 1985).
13. "AMD Grabs Market Share from Intel," *Information Week*, June 10, 2009.
14. In discussion with Professor Liang Neng, at CEIBS, May 2005.
15. Resource integration ability refers to the firms' ability to redeploy resources to maximize global synergies; for example, move European and American plants to China, be it the key components of global procurement or raw materials.

Galanz's cooperation with multinational companies is also a kind of resource integration; that is, to agglomerate the manufacturing capacity of two sides to China while, at the same time, sharing sales channels around the world. But this integration is beyond the bounds of a single firm.

16. Hemerling, Michael and Michaelis, 2006.
17. "China Spreads Its Wings—Chinese companies Go Global," Accenture Publications, 2005.
18. Citigroup Research, *European Portfolio Strategist*, December 3, 2008.
19. In an interview with the authors.
20. Phillip L. Zweig, "The Case against Mergers," *BusinessWeek*, October 30, 1995.
21. Quoted in Richard M. DiGeorgio: "Making Mergers and Acquisitions Work: What We Know and Don't Know—Part I." *Journal of Change Management* 2(2) (December 2002): 134–48.
22. Zhen Wang, Biaoyan Sun and Xiaoyan Zhang, "Exclusive Interview of Dongsheng Li: Globalization is the Greatest Challenge in My Career Life," *First Financial Daily*, August 31, 2005.

People First: Building Global Competence

Finding, assessing, and developing talents add up to 60–70 percent of my time. That's the key to success

Jack Welch[1]

Organizational Capability: An Overview

Competing for an Olympic medal takes decades of dedication and hard training. In August 2008, China showed the world that it was ready to live up to Olympia's high standards. Its athletes won a total of 100 medals, including 51 gold. For the Chinese government and people, the Olympic events, as well as the medals won by the Chinese athletes, were a great source of national pride, for it was China's opportunity to show the world its achievements, old and new.

Similar to the hosting of the Olympic Games, globalization relies on solid strength—the company's organizational capability. After defining global strategy and choosing the proper globalization path, Chinese firms must break through the "concrete ceiling" of organizational capability if they are to become global leaders. Organizational capability is acquired through long-term competition, learning, and continuous improvement. A successful company should have excellent organizational capabilities that are suited to its strategy.

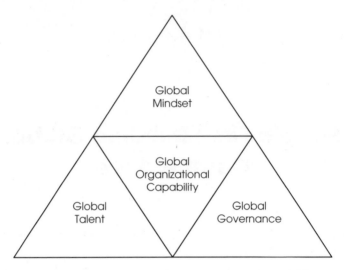

Figure 5.1   Framework of Global Organizational Capability

The successes of Chinese firms in the home market are backed by solid strength. Many of these companies have shown that they can also adjust or build new capabilities according to their global strategic needs when they go abroad. Figure 5.1 introduces a framework for Chinese firms, centered on three pillars of global organizational capability: global talent, global mindset, and global management method.

As mentioned in Chapter 1, these three pillars are mutually supporting, balanced, and indispensable.

Global talent

The first step towards globalization is having global talent (staff who have global knowledge, ability, and quality), especially management talent. Specific questions to be considered in this regard include:

- What abilities and qualities for global leadership should headquarters and branch staff have?
- How should such talent be introduced, promoted, and developed within the company?
- How can the company go about building a global talent pool and optimize its human resources on a global scale?

- How can cross-cultural teams be managed effectively in order to promote mutual trust and synergies?

Global mindset

International companies have branches all over the world, with employees from different cultural backgrounds. Their shared values and ethics determine the company's overall competitiveness. Specific questions to be answered relate to:

- How to build and implement a diversified yet performance-oriented global culture. What are the effective mechanisms and methods for this?
- How to handle cultural conflicts and optimize synergistic effects.
- How to develop a performance-management system that suits an international organization. How can the company balance global consistency with local differences?
- How to develop an incentive system that suits an international organization.

Global governance

Companies should provide an effective management system that allows talented employees to enrich themselves in implementing the global strategies. Specific questions that need to be worked on relate to:

- How to design a structure that supports the company's global strategy.
- How to balance the centralization of power in integrating global resources while being open to local business opportunities.
- How to optimize the distribution of knowledge and innovation in a global organization.
- How to build an information system that supports global operations. What information is to be managed globally?

    The emphasis required on each of these three pillars will vary in accordance with the company's global strategic positioning and path, depending on its choice as local market competitor, global resource user, local market explorer, or global market player.

Shortage of Global Talent

According to Jack Welch: "Talent is foremost. The organization is right when you get the right people."[2] To realize its globalizing strategy, the company should first of all have the right people; that is, a number of people who meet its strategic needs. Whatever their nationality and cultural background, global leadership personnel should have global vision, intercultural communication, and management skills, and the ability to integrate international resources. Christopher Bartlett of Harvard Business School and Sumantra Ghoshal of the London Business School, both authorities in international companies, point out that transnational companies need four types of specialties: business managers, who further the company's global scale efficiency and competitiveness; country managers, who are sensitive and responsive to the local market; functional managers, who can use learning to create and spread innovations and transfer specialized knowledge, while also connecting scarce resources and capabilities across national borders; and top executives at corporate headquarters, who manage the complex interactions between the three and can identify and develop the talented executives a successful transnational requires. They believe that: "A company's ability to identify individuals with potential, legitimize their diversity, and integrate them into the organization's corporate decisions is the single clearest indicator that the corporate leader is a true global manager, and that the company is a true transnational."[3] A diversity of top executives with international working experience is common in mature international companies. With the company's globalization, the number of non-American senior executives in GE increased from 16 percent in 2004 to 25 percent in 2006.[4] In Caterpillar, the world leader in mechanical engineering, 30 of its 36 top executives have worked overseas.[5] Almost all senior executives in international companies such as IBM, Shell, and P&G have had international working experience.

As latecomers, Chinese firms face special challenges in obtaining talent with the necessary experience for global operations.

Talent shortage

According to a McKinsey survey in 2005, only 10 percent of Chinese college graduates meet the requirements of international companies because of factors relating to language, communication, and culture.[6] In the next 10 to 15 years, Chinese companies will need 75,000 global managers, but have a talent pool of only 3,000 to 5,000 at their disposal at present. The shortage of global talent has forced many Chinese firms to abandon or postpone their globalization plans, or entrust several projects to just a handful of people, increasing the likelihood of costly mistakes.

As a result of the financial crisis, many Chinese financial institutions have had the opportunity to recruit foreign talent—a move supported and encouraged by the city of Shanghai's intention to build a Chinese Wall Street. Also, the recruitment of new MBA students has shown a marked increase in the number of applicants from the United States. For example, from 2008 to 2010 about 30 percent of participants in CEIBS programs were drawn from foreign nationals, ABC (American-born Chinese) and Chinese students from Western financial institutions. Many of these students come with the hope of finding promising job opportunities in China after graduation.

Lack of professional management ability

Globalization means not just dealing with global customers, competitors and suppliers, but also facing the challenges brought by a more complicated organization (large scale, cultural diversity, and multiple departments). However, compared to their counterparts in international companies, talented employees in Chinese firms tend to be more entrepreneurial than professional. Individualistic heroism prevails over standardized management procedures, for two main reasons.

First, there is no system for developing talent. Many Chinese firms are too busy meeting challenges to set up talent-development programs. Talented individuals, who emerge as "firefighters," have neither systematic training, nor cross-functional and cross-regional practice. Although there can be some superstars, the abilities of team members are by no means evenly distributed.

Second, Chinese entrepreneurs are too deeply influenced by the characteristics of the Chinese market and culture. In a business environment full of opportunities and changing regulations, Chinese entrepreneurs are short-term oriented, swift, and dynamic. Many of them work in several positions: they are street-smart in making use of connections and regulations, but are short of experience in intensive management and in setting up standardized procedures and systems. Their management can be useful in similar emerging markets, but inadequate in mature ones. This management gap becomes evident when Chinese firms attempt the acquisition and integration of Western companies.

Disadvantages in attracting talent

International companies are usually perceived to be attractive employers because of their strength, reputation, and mature training programs. This has been proven in the Chinese market. According to research conducted by Manpower Inc.: "Foreign MNCs operating in China have an edge on local organizations competing for talent. Nearly 75 percent of Chinese employees prefer to work for wholly-owned foreign companies rather than joint ventures or wholly-owned Chinese companies."[7]

Nevertheless, Chinese firms can still take measures to deal with the shortage of global talent. Chinese companies such as Lenovo, Haier, Huawei, CIMC, Acer, and Trend Micro have shown that it is possible to develop and introduce global talent to support the effective implementation of their global strategies.

Starting from the Top

The implementation of important business decisions must be recognized and supported by the company's leadership; breaking through the shortage of global talent is no exception. Top executives, especially CEOs, should take the lead in attracting, developing, and maintaining global talent, in enlarging the leadership's global horizon, in improving their inter-cultural communication and management skills, and in integrating global resources. This is particularly important for Chinese firms, which are weak in procedures and systems. According to our research, leaders of successful global Chinese firms share the following common features.

Global horizon and strategic vision

Leaders of these Chinese firms have the global vision to explore resources and opportunities all over the world, predict international industry trends, position their companies in the global value chain, and set objectives for their companies.

Training global talent

Fully realizing the importance of talent to the company's globalization, they balance short-term profit and long-term development needs effectively, take the lead in improving their global vision and inter-cultural management ability, and commit themselves to attracting and training global talent.

Open-mindedness and learning ability

Good leaders are willing to place talented individuals from different cultural backgrounds in senior positions in branches overseas as well as in headquarters. These leaders are very capable of listening to different ideas and gaining knowledge from other talented people within the company, from external experts, and even from competitors.

Institutionalization

Effective leaders focus on building the company's infrastructure, laying the foundations for development, and establishing organizational structures, responsibilities, and procedures.

Ambition and perseverance

The path toward globalization can be perilous and even industry leaders have to work extremely hard to maintain their position. Ambitious, unyielding and aware of risks, they elevate their companies into even higher stages.

Mai Boliang, president of CIMC, is one such visionary leader. Since taking the position as general manager of CIMC in the early 1990s, he has transformed the company into the global leader of the container industry, attaining a market share of more than 50 percent—and this during a period of industrial downturn. Since then, and with due consideration to its core competence, CIMC has diversified its activities into providing equipment and services for the transportation industry. In these activities, it has made full use of experienced local talent, particularly in its activities in the United States.

With design centers, manufacturing bases and trading companies in more than 30 countries, Haier is now a real international company. Realizing that Chinese firms were being outpaced by their peers, not just in technology but, more importantly, in management abilities, its CEO, Zhang Ruimin, has focused on establishing effective corporate systems. His aim is to ensure that Haier is managed by a sustainable system instead of men, to the effect that Haier's leaders in the future can see a bigger picture and make better decisions with global vision."[8] Haier took pains to rebuild its procedures and to promote innovation in marketing and technology. Zhang Ruimin is also open to learning. He visits branches, at home and abroad, every year and listens to frontline workers to get to know how the company is running. He also learns from other international companies:

> GE is not the only one we can learn from. We learn the spirit of innovation from American companies, and team spirit from the Japanese, such as Honda, who have the best team management in the world. From Korean companies, we learn the spirit of enterprise. . . . I think that there's always something we can learn from companies who survive, no matter where they are from.[9]

Stan Shih, former chairman of Acer, is another who was willing to open his company to global thinking, knowing that Acer, as a global company, could not afford to be limited to or by a Taiwanese mindset. He explained his thinking this way: "Since Acer's going global in 1989, my idea is that talent is borderless. For Chinese firms playing on the international stage, integration of only Chinese resources is far from enough. We need the cooperation of foreigners to integrate global resources."[10]

Lenovo is another company that has shown through its actions in appointing foreign CEOs and leading managers that it recognizes and respects the skills and experience required for it to become fully integrated in global activities.

Steve Chang, founder of Trend Micro, makes the effort to speak English (because he thinks foreigners find Chinese too difficult to learn), and was the first president of a Japanese company who didn't speak Japanese. Yet Trend Micro operates well in Japan, which accounts for 40 percent of its global revenue. Also known as "Mr. Change," Chang insists on three things: technology innovation, international operation, and a self-owned brand. When he realized that the company needed professionals to improve its management structures, he didn't hesitate to introduce talented, experienced foreigners into his leadership team, which now includes talent drawn from six countries. He also interviews candidates for key positions in person. But attracting talent is just the start; bringing their abilities into full play is more challenging. When he was the CEO, Chang took the lead in actively changing the decision-making model into one based on "team consensus" to take full advantage of the global talent at his disposal.

Fittest is Best

Companies should first define the qualities they are looking for in the people they wish to recruit and train. Generally, the more global resources the company has and the more markets it operates in, the higher the quality of the talent it needs (see Figure 5.2).

Chinese companies competing with international companies in the home market are not in such urgent need of global talent because their success depends on having locals who know the domestic market well. Chinese firms competing with counterparts both at home and abroad by using global resources in the home market need global talent in key fields. For example, Li Ning and Pearl River Piano both hired foreign designers. Chinese companies exploring markets abroad should find people who know local business practices, marketing channels, and customers. For instance, CIMC, Pearl River Piano, and Midea entered overseas market with the help of local personnel and partners. Global operators such as Lenovo, Haier, TCL-Thomson, Huawei, ZTE, and Trend Micro all need global talent as business managers, country managers, functional managers, and top executives.

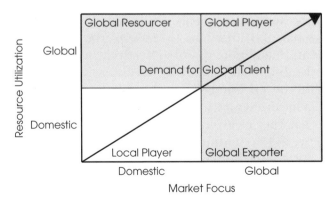

Figure 5.2　Global Strategic Focus and Talent Requirement

A company's need for global talent varies according to the particular globalization path it has chosen. Those who choose strategic alliances need people capable of negotiating and coordinating operations with their partners. Companies that go global via organic growth can introduce and train managers to work overseas gradually, in line with their globalization schedule. And for those realizing globalization through M&A, the key factor is the ability of their Chinese executives to maintain, encourage, and use global talent.

Warren Buffett once said: "If you have capable managers, even if you are managing a dozen of them or more, you still have time to doze."[11] For companies operating globally, these managers should be capable, trustworthy, and comply with all aspects of the company's core values. Finding the right global talent is essential to ensure healthy growth of global businesses. Answering the following questions can be helpful in guaranteeing that companies are on the right track.

Do staff capabilities meet our global strategic needs?   Companies should define and review the expertise and skills of the employees on the basis of their global strategy. In addition to acquired expertise, key staff should be open to taking on new knowledge and up-to-date skills demanded by globalization.

Do employees identify with our company culture and are they adaptable to a multicultural environment?   While one of the advantages of globalization is the access it gives to global talent, it is only when their values and ethics are in accord with the company's culture that they become assets to the company. Although headquarters can ensure the compliance of employees working overseas via performance appraisals, regulation is not perfect. Indeed, many companies have no idea how to evaluate the value of new introduced talent. In addition, to work effectively in a multicultural environment, leading staff should be culturally sensitive and respect cultural differences. The best may be able to implement corporate culture in a localized way.

CIMC has very clear criteria in recruiting global talent. As set out in Figure 5.3, in addition to expertise and experience in their specialist areas and the ability to apply these in a global context, potential recruits will identify with CIMC's corporate culture, core values, and long-term objectives.

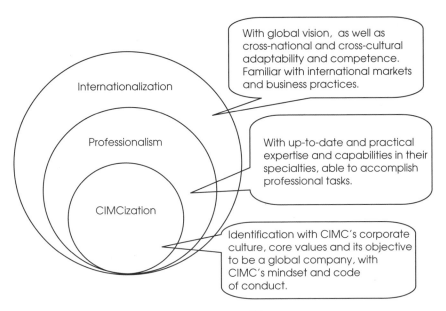

Figure 5.3   CIMC's Recruitment Criteria[12]

What do our staff need? Can the company meet their needs? Companies should know the factors that motivate and sustain talented employees. For example, to compete with top international companies for the globally experienced staff it needs, Li Ning offers a platform for rapid development in a sports environment.

Are our executives willing to accept and able to manage talented individuals?   The fresh ideas that new recruits with global experience bring with them do not always meet with the approval of a company's existing executives. If executives are reluctant to accept these new ideas and practices, the company may have difficulty in retaining its international talent.

In Haier's businesses overseas, the common practice is to hire experienced people from leading white-goods companies to be country heads entrusted with developing local management teams and establishing sales channels. Haier's stated aim is "meeting customers' needs with local mentalities and by local people." When it began its U.S. operations in 1999, 16 of its 17 employees were non-Chinese. And when its European branch was set up in 2000, the general manager was an Italian with vast experience of the industry in Europe. In India, the general manager was a former executive from Whirlpool India.[13]

From its early days, Huawei itself set the goal of "becoming a leading telecommunication equipment supplier in the world." It targeted top college graduates from top universities, and it assigned the best employees to explore markets abroad. To attract, encourage, and maintain such talent, Huawei provides the best salary and benefits in the industry. Galanz, on the other hand, favors "smart heads from humble families." In keeping with its low-cost strategy, when recruiting overseas it employs people who meet its requirements on a project basis rather than on permanent contracts. The contrasting strategies of these two companies have one thing in common, though: survival of the fittest!

Preparing for the Future

Companies have a variety of channels open to them from which to recruit the people they need to fulfill their global ambitions. Each of these channels has its advantages and disadvantages, as set out in Table 5.1.

Table 5.1   Channels for recruiting global talent

	Recruitment	Training	Merger	Borrowing
Advantages	Speed Diversity	Solid development High level of cultural compatibility	Speed Large quantity	Speed Low cost
Disadvantages	Low level of cultural compatibility	Slow Costly	Low level of cultural compatibility Costly Difficulty in cultural integration	Small quantity Short employment

Recruitment

When expanding overseas it is necessary to employ locals who know the market and are more familiar with the resources available. While this is a common practice among international companies operating in China, many Chinese firms are reluctant to hire foreign executives. It is all a matter of time and trust, as Stan Shih pointed out: "At the beginning, Acer was in trouble with foreign executives, and vice versa. The establishment of mutual trust required not only performance from foreigners but also support from Acer."[14]

Guangxi's Liugong Machinery Co., Ltd. has enjoyed great success in its overseas recruitment efforts thanks, in no small way, to the personal influence of its president, Zeng Guang'an. Zeng, who is fluent in English, maintains close ties with companies overseas and is able to put these personal connections to good use when it comes to finding people capable of helping the company fulfill its global strategy. That's how he found the general manager of Liugong's branch in Australia, for example, who also recommended others with the skills and experience Liugong was seeking. Recruitment built on close business relationships is likely to be based on mutual understanding and respect.

Steve Chang at Trend Micro also stays in contact with people he meets through business or international conferences and invites them to join Trend Micro when required (see Appendix 7).

Any company looking to recruit talent, from at home or overseas, must have the following in place:

- *Training:* This is a very competitive area between companies. International companies with many years of consistent success, such as GE and IBM, establish in-house systems for training new recruits to support their (both company and recruit) continuous growth.
- *Drive from the leadership:* To support Huawei's globalization, Ren Zhengfei set preferential reward and promotion policies for employees with proven experience working in underdeveloped regions overseas.[15] Working on the basis that "The tougher the environment, the faster they will grow," he also asks department heads for recommendations for people to work overseas. Ren's emphasis on the company's talent strategy has been crucial in Huawei's expansion overseas.

- *Explicit requirement of talents:* As we saw earlier, CIMC has specific recruitment criteria. Lenovo, the pioneer in China's push for globalization, evaluates potential recruits on performance, proficiency, potential, and professionalism (see Appendix 8).
- *Classroom training:* Global recruits generally spend up to 20 percent of their total training time in the classroom, which incorporates language learning, courses on transnational operations and trans-cultural management at business schools, and in-house training run by company executives.
- *Work-and-learn:* Some 80 percent of training comes through on-the-job practice. Companies going global via organic growth can provide trans-cultural working opportunities for their employees. Employees in Trend Micro and BenQ, for example, are able to rotate through different locations, functions, and departments. When they return, they are required to share their experiences of cultural differences, and how they coped with the various challenges that confronted them.
- *Assessment mechanisms:* Key performance indices should be agreed on so that senior executives can review and discuss the recruits' progress and identify points for improvement.
- Training global talent takes time and money. In international companies such as GE, IBM, and ABB, talent-training plans are conducted on a long-term basis using a step-by-step approach. If Chinese firms fail to set up appropriate training systems for potential global talent, their hopes of becoming a global leader will remain in the realms of fantasy.

Merger

Talented individuals can also be acquired through mergers and there are many examples to illustrate how effective this can be. For example, Gianfranco Lanci joined Acer from Texas Instruments (TI) when Acer acquired TI's laptop business in 1997. In 2005, Lanci became Acer's global general manager.

With the acquisition of IBM's PC business, Lenovo inherited 1,800 excellent R&D and management staff. Former IBM staff took half of the top positions in Lenovo's global structure. These decisions reflect not only business needs, but also Lenovo's resolution to be a real global company. Qiao Jiao, vice-president of the company's global human resources, has said that Lenovo is open "to new knowledge and practices" and acknowledged that "due diligence, decision-making and cooperation with foreign executives and consulting companies are all best opportunities to learn."[16]

Borrowing

Hiring external talent (such as external counselors) for specific needs is another way of making good use of available global talent. By working with external counselors in areas such as due diligence, legal negotiation, and integrating compensation and benefits, company staff can gain valuable experience and expertise outside of their usual activities.

Summary

The realization of globalization starts with obtaining staff with the necessary experience and expertise to see it through. This is a universal truth acknowledged by international companies everywhere. Attempting to undertake the process without the necessary human resources leads only to waste and failure.

The varied experiences of the likes of Huawei, Lenovo, Haier, and CIMC over the past two decades underline the importance of selecting and grooming global leadership talent. They have a lot to teach the leaders of other Chinese companies about the need to be open-minded when it comes to taking on new ideas and practices.

Endnotes

1. Jack Welch, "How to Be a Talent Magnet," *BusinessWeek*, September 11, 2006.
2. Ibid.
3. Barlett and Ghoshal, 2003: 101–08.
4. Barlett, 2006: 1.
5. "Moving Caterpillar from Good to Great, an Interview with Jim Owens," *InterBusiness Issues*, Peroria Magazines, December 2005.
6. Dianna Farrell and Andrew J. Grant, "China's Looming Talent Shortage," *The McKinsey Quarterly* 4, 2005: 70.
7. Joerres, 2007.
8. Zhang Ruimin in an interview with CEIBS.
9. Ke En, "The Ultimate Goal of Leadership: An Interview with Zhang Ruimin," *Harvard Business Review* (Chinese Version), January 2007.
10. Wang Qi, "Stan Shih: Foreign Head is Not Accidental," *Chinese Entrepreneurs* 11, 2005: 42.
11. "Buffett's Wisdom," *Management Digest* (Fortune Chinese Version), April 2005: 130.

12. Based on a speech by Wu Fapei, vice-president of CIMC, during a Forum of Chinese Firms Going Global held by China Europe International Business School in February 2006.

13. Krishna Palepu, Tarun Khanna and Ingrid Vargas, "Haier: Taking a Chinese Company Global," Harvard Business School cases, August 25, 2006: 12–14.

14. Wang Qi, op. cit.: 43.

15. Wen Liyan, *Human Resource Management in Huawei* (Seasky Publishing House, 2006, 82–83).

16. Qiao Jiao during the conference "Leading China's Future, Future Chinese Leaders," November 26, 2006, CEIBS.

Unity in Diversity: Shaping a Global Mindset

*The only way to realize cohesion within the company is to win
hearts with a universal corporate culture.*

Steve Chang

Cultural Differences: Blessing or Curse?

"Everything changed all of a sudden. I'm not used to the TCL
way. A sense of insecurity has been permeating the office from
day one of the acquisition. Besides orders and operation, the
most obvious change is the salary system. T&A is adopting
TCL's incentive model, which means the new salary system is
much more sales sensitive than the Alcatel one."

**Former Alcatel employee following TCL's
acquisition of Alcatel's mobile business.**[1]

"Price control is the key to mobile-phone sales; high prices can be
demanded with new product launches. German product development cannot keep up with the demands of customers. With prices
down 15 to 20 percent each quarter, how can we make a profit?"

**K. Y. Lee, as BenQ announced its abandonment
of Siemens' mobile business.**[2]

101

"Communication is important in the service industry. In Trend Micro, we never know who will be working with us and what their cultural backgrounds are because this is a highly globalized company. These work experiences make us increasingly skillful in communication."

Trend Micro employee when asked how he was benefiting from inter-cultural communications.[3]

"With the implementation of the management and distribution system, employees in the Schiess GmbH branch have to work 10 percent longer a week, and get paid according to their workload. This is quite unexpected, considering the importance placed on leisure time in European and German culture. What's more, this was something that the German managers proposed. It's the embodiment of Schiess' success in combining Chinese and German cultures."

Chen Huiren, President, SMTCL, after the company's German acquisition.[4]

For better or worse, the influx of foreign goods into China has been accompanied by foreign cultures. Cultural differences accounted (at least partially) for the failure of some of the major acquisitions we examined in earlier chapters.

Others have fared better, of course, as the quotes set out above clearly indicate. However, given the contrasting nature of the responses recorded above, we can't help but ponder: Is cultural difference a blessing or a curse? What cultural challenges will Chinese firms face as they go global? How can they overcome these challenges to become leading players in the world?

Cultural Challenges for Chinese Firms

Strategic alliance, organic growth, or M&A—no matter which path to globalization is chosen, culture shock is inevitable. However, the degree of impact can vary. Galanz chose the strategic-alliance path to avoid potential culture conflicts over such things as foreign employees' attitudes to working overtime, the possibility of strikes, and so on. Organic growth enables companies to decide the speed of their expansion overseas and to reduce risks in transnational operations. For example, TCL operated well in emerging markets such as Vietnam and the Philippines before they began making acquisitions. Similarly, BenQ had built a very solid revenue base in Europe prior to its acquisitions.

M&A is the most intense and obvious source of culture shock. Participants tend to be blinded by the rather simplistic notion of instant synergies ("1+1=2"), overlooking potential troubles caused by cultural differences which can undermine that notion. In most successful M&A cases, a strong company acquires a weaker one.

Short of globalization experience, Chinese firms tend to underestimate the challenges posed by trans-cultural acquisition and are quickly confronted by the dilemma of which model to adopt— whether to impose the Chinese model or adopt that of the acquired company. Either way, a consideration of the cultural factors involved is essential to the integration of talent, business, and structure.

Different cultures within TTE

TCL-Thomson Electrics (TTE) has had to deal with several cultures ever since its establishment in 2004. It has had to find a way of accommodating and blending Chinese, North American and European values and attitudes into its approach to business. It took time for Chinese employees and those returning from overseas to get accustomed to each other's ideas, let alone the differences in thinking and pace between Chinese and foreigners. Coming from a mature Western market, Thomson attached importance to systems and procedures, while TCL believed in flexibility and personal motivation to fit the rapidly changing Chinese market. Li Dongsheng framed the early problems this way: "When people from TCL were eager to take action, their Thomson co-workers were still working on procedures."

There are profound differences between the Chinese, French, and American cultures that are evident when looking at attitudes toward work and loyalty to the company:

- **Attitudes toward work:** Considering work as an important part of their life, Chinese are willing to work overtime. Americans are also inclined to finish their work before relaxation, but French people believe work is not more important than leisure time. It is difficult to convince them to work overtime.

- **Loyalty to company:** Chinese employees strongly identify with the company and accept less compensation when the company is not running well. Western employees believe that the CEO is responsible for revenue, and they are entitled to their benefits (bonus and vacation) if they are doing well individually.

The integration of salary systems is another challenge. Even when the Chinese company is profitable while the foreign company is not, Chinese employees are generally paid less than their overseas counterparts and the usual compensations and benefits that international employees enjoy are often far out of the reach of Chinese employees.

TTE had anticipated that it would be profitable within 18 months of the completion of the acquisition. But cultural differences and technological challenges hindered its integration to the point where it could not realize the expected synergistic effects. It ended up closing all sales and marketing businesses in OEM and restructuring its European operations.

The BenQ-Siemens cultural nightmare

If TTE's story is surprising, BenQ's acquisition of Siemens is even more astonishing. Before the deal, BenQ had had substantial experience in global operations, and some of its leadership had worked or studied overseas. Executives from the two companies had exchanged ideas before the deal and were happy to find that they had some understanding of each other's cultures. K. Y. Lee appointed the former head of the Cordless Product Division of Siemens Mobile as CEO, and two senior executives from BenQ as President and CFO. Unfortunately, things didn't turn out according to BenQ's expectations. Siemens was still processing internal applications manually because the labor union was concerned that computerization would lead to layoffs. Because of this, there was a two-month lag in its financial data, and the massive outsourcing of R&D caused difficulties with management and coordination. Without the pace they needed for survival, they were unable to produce the expected synergies. R&D in new products slowed right down—a fatal blow in the mobile industry.

Moreover, employees in BenQ's Beijing R&D center did not feel integrated in the first year of acquisition. Siemens' R&D staff in Germany, Shanghai, and Beijing still operated in the same old way, while those from BenQ's Taipei, Hsinchu, and Suzhou centers worked on their own, without much communication with their Siemens counterparts. R&D staff from Siemens believed that these two companies' ideas toward R&D were polar opposites. BenQ emphasized short-term markets and had different concepts and ideas in design, which were rarely discussed with Siemens.[5] Finally, Lee was forced to admit to the inherent differences between BenQ and Siemens:

> Siemens' culture is one of engineers and technologies, centered on risk control and budget, while Asian firms emphasize innovation and flexibility. Enterprising Asian firms adjust their budget in line with need, but employees from Siemens insist on spending only the budget that has been approved, be it necessary or not.[6]

In Asian companies such as BenQ, working overtime is commonplace when needed, but this is not so in Germany. Opposition from the powerful labor union meant that the planned move of German factories to the Czech Republic had to be postponed for 18 months. Belatedly, BenQ finally realized that the acquisition would not work; with heavy losses, uncontrollable factors, and pressure, K. Y. Lee had no choice but to pull the plug.[7]

Lessons learned

TCL and BenQ embodied the management characteristics of Chinese companies: an emphasis on speed and flexibility and making decisions according to intuition rather than statistics. These characteristics did bring them successes both at home and abroad, and local executives in BenQ Europe appreciated BenQ leadership's trade experiences and loyalty to the company. However, with Siemens, BenQ was stifled because the European giant was larger in scale, and more mature in its management systems. Its practice of sticking to procedures and statistics, slow decision-making, and implementation as well as meeting needs in the market, were not what BenQ could work with.

Such cultural differences may prove less challenging if the chosen path is one of organic growth or strategic alliance, but with

M&A, where synergies have to be realized, culture shock has more powerful effects. Needless to say, before going ahead with an acquisition companies should have a solid understanding of cultural differences and be prepared for any potential problems that could arise from them.

In addition to cultural and management challenges, another important factor to be considered is the globalization of the salary system, which is an essential tool for encouraging and shaping corporate values. With the expansion of branches overseas, companies need to be able to balance global consistency and local diversity. Poor management of the salary system will hurt the performance of employees, whether they are executives or entry-level staff.

Bridging Culture Gaps

The culture of a globalized company must be able to serve its business objectives: seizing global opportunities, utilizing global resources, and bringing sustained growth. Eventual success is determined by the players' ability to explore and make effective use of opportunities and resources. This is why companies must have staff who have expertise, knowledge of local resources, and an ability to work in different markets and regions with ease and skill. A corporate culture that attracts, fosters, motivates, and maintains talent is open, tolerant, and has universal core values based on performance.

Cultural tolerance means having respect for cultural diversity and an understanding of local traditions and conventions that have an impact on the workplace (for example, the need to respect Muslims' prayer times). All of this requires cultural sensitivity. When entering the semi-trailer platform in the American market, CIMC appointed local people to run the factories to show its respect for local culture, while headquarters supported them in purchasing and technology. It has proven to be a good way of doing business.

But cultural tolerance alone is not enough. As Stan Shih has pointed out: "Corporate culture speaks through business performance."[8] Below are examples of the many foreign international companies that have been successful in managing cultural differences.

GE Capital

This company is something of an M&A expert, acquiring some 50 companies during the European economic slowdown of 1989–1995,

16 companies within six months when Mexico's currency depreciated in 1995, and making similar deals in Japan during the Asian financial crisis in 1997. These successful trans-cultural acquisitions are supported by its mature acquisition and integration system. GE Capital uses a variety of management tools to promote mutual understanding of culture and realization of business targets, such as cultural brain-storming, joint projects, and training of overseas managers at headquarters.

Renault-Nissan Strategic Alliance

Although the market was not optimistic about the strategic alliance of Renault and Nissan, the cooperation turned out to be a success. One of the reasons for this was that executives from both companies had established a rapport before the alliance. In the spirit of "equality and joint management" set by Renault, senior executives set a good example for the staff of both companies, with Renault appointing a former senior executive from Nissan as a senior vice-president. The success of the venture was achieved around reaching a balance between Japanese and French management methods and an exchange of management skills and best practices, rather than through a cultural merger. Besides respecting their cultural differences, the companies also reached consensus on such things as quality, cost, and delivery.

ABB

Formed in 1988 from the merger of two international engineering companies—the Swiss BBC company and the Swedish ASEA—ABB acquired more than 230 companies in 50 countries within a decade. It didn't build its corporate culture on that of its parent countries, but on its diversity. The core of its management philosophy was to respect local culture and acculturation. English is the language of management at ABB, even at its headquarters in Switzerland, where there are employees from 19 countries. The company is led by managers who know the local culture and the company's global strategy. ABB spends almost US$1 billion annually on management training, and research into trans-cultural communications.[9]

As in the examples above, successful global Chinese firms have accumulated experience in trans-cultural management. They have established core values that are clear, globally consistent, and supportive of their strategy implementation goals.

Building a Global Culture

Companies going global should define a set of core values that are performance-oriented, globally consistent, and designed to enhance trans-cultural communication and coordination. There are three aspects to this, as illustrated in Figure 6.1.

Clear definitions

Establishing defined and globally consistent core values is the first step in shaping and building a global culture. These values embody the common principles and ethics of the company, and are above and beyond any nationalistic sentiments. They are universal values established by the company's senior management and should be communicated and shared across the entire organization. They should be interpreted in light of the local culture to avoid misunderstanding. For example, what is meant by trust and respect? In China, trust and respect may mean picking you up at the airport, showing you around the cities, and spending time with you with a wonderful banquet. In the United States, trust and respect may mean different sets of behaviors. It is important to define those specific meanings and behaviors in a local context though the company core values are universal.

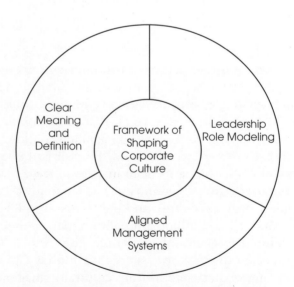

Figure 6.1   A Framework for Shaping Corporate Culture

Take Trend Micro, for example. Operating in 30 countries, Trend Micro's revenues in 2008 amounted to US$850 million, 90 percent of which came from Japan, Europe, the U.S., and Latin America.

Without establishing core values and ethical standards, a company operating in a multicultural environment cannot hope to provide the best services or products to its global clients. What holds Trend Micro together are its core values (which it refers to as "4C+1T"—change, creativity, communications, customer, and trustworthiness).

Two communication principles are promoted within Trend Micro to smooth inter-cultural communications: "No ego"—which prioritizes the needs of the company over those of the individual—and "Be you, be the best of yourself"—which encourages everyone to be true to themselves when working in a team.

A new corporate culture should be developed to bridge the culture gaps that can sometimes occur with mergers and acquisitions. For instance, when Lenovo took over IBM's PC business there were both corporate and national cultural differences to contend with. The company listened to executives and employees from both sides to arrive at a set of core values that would guide its activities. These comprised:

- Service—strive for customer satisfaction and success
- Innovation—pursue efficiency and innovation
- Integrity—establish trust and responsible interpersonal relationships
- Diversity—promote mutual understanding, respect diversity, and perceive culture with a global vision.

To promote mutual understanding, Lenovo has a website where employees can post their queries—Should I adopt an English name? Should I argue with my foreign boss?—and have them answered by co-workers or experts. In this way, executives know what employees' concerns are, and can take appropriate measures to bridge cultural gaps.

For companies who make strategic alliances with foreign firms, developing shared principles and values of cooperation among the business partners is most fundamental to successful collaboration. SAIC's partnership strategy is two-pronged: "Coming-in—attracting partners for win-win success in the China market; Going-out—integrating resources to capture global opportunities." Making

these partnership strategies work entails several partnership principles, such as striving to speak with one voice: that is, seeking the
same objectives at the same pace in such a way that everyone benefits. Leaders of both companies commit to work out solutions
together for mutual success. They study each other's cultures and
conventions to promote mutual understanding and trust. They set
up joint committees to set and follow a standardized approach to
decisions on such things as quality, price, and service. They are flexible
but pragmatic in their dealings with each other and the interests of
the joint-venture company always come first.[10]

Building upon such partnership principles, SAIC has succeeded
in establishing 70 joint ventures (15 of which are with companies
ranked within the world's top 500). Such has been its success that
its sales revenues have increased 84-fold in two decades and it even
has its own brand, Roewe, a symbol of its increased management
ability and strength.

Leaders as role models

It is one thing for companies to have core values, but implementing
them is quite another. According to our research, successful implementation of core values is determined by the example set by the leadership and the supporting system. The example set by senior executives
is embodied in their behavior, decision-making, and time allocation.

As Jenny Chen of Trend Micro sees it: "Culture cannot be something institutional—that would be dull and lifeless. We prefer continuous activity every day. Brands can be built with money, but this
is not how culture works."[11]

With this in mind, the company began by focusing on regular
company meetings. "It was not just us," Chen explains, "but all leaders in the company who were to meet employees as often as possible."
Trend Micro requires that the cohesion between company executives
is even stronger than that with their subordinates. There is daily communication via email and teleconference, and face-to-face quarterly
meetings to ensure that every employee's target is in "total alignment"
with the company's mission, strategy, and core values.

Chen and Steve Chang, the founders of Trend Micro, spend
two-thirds of their time on traveling to promote corporate culture.
The beneficial effects of this are felt across the organization, as one
human-resources executive explains:

I had worked in foreign-invested companies before and was curious why corporate culture is so strong in Trend Micro [and] how corporate culture could be so far-reaching. One of the reasons is the example set by Steve Chang, Eva Chen, and Jenny Chen. The consistency of their words and actions is very persuasive and is as well received by employees as their work ethic. . . . [T]hey find that it is very easy to identify with Trend Micro because of its global vision.[12]

Supporting management system

Culture becomes rooted in the company only when it is filtered into every aspect of daily work.

In Trend Micro, "customer first" is more than just a slogan. In 2004, project teams were sent to talk to customers in different regions. When they found that customers' needs differ not regionally but according to segments—such as corporations, SMEs, and individuals—Trend Micro changed its strategy and organizational structure so that R&D and marketing were geared toward meeting the needs of these various segments.

Trend Micro's recruitment and performance-assessment strategies are also centered around its core values. It attaches great importance to candidates' compatibility with its culture and applicants for senior executive positions are interviewed by the company's founders and have to undergo rigorous IQ and EQ assessments. Employees at every level have to be highly responsible and self-disciplined and their performance is assessed against values that are applied consistently across the entire organization. In this regard, business ethics are considered just as seriously as business performance: one business manager in Central America who was found to be padding his expenses was fired, despite his otherwise excellent performance.

Sometimes, work practices that are successful in one culture may not translate well to another. Haier, for example, found that it had to make adjustments to its expectations as it established itself in the United States. In China, Haier punishes employees who perform badly by making deductions from their salary; similar poor performance by U.S. employees meets with suspension from work. In China, the day's worst-performing worker or manager has to analyze the reasons for this in public, while in the U.S., it is only those with the best performance that share their experience openly. CIMC has also changed American practice to ensure performance. For example, it has reduced the number of times (from seven/ eight to three) that employees can be absent from work without good reason before they are fired.

For M&A companies, the subject of compensation and benefits across the organization can cause difficulties unless measures are in place to ensure that the system for determining remuneration packages is consistent and equitable. To prevent potential conflict in this area, Lenovo has instituted a three-step process for determining remuneration and benefits in both IBM and Lenovo. This puts people into different categories according to their responsibilities, business influence, communication requirements, and employee coverage. It also makes determinations according to whether people at the same level have international responsibilities and whether these responsibilities are within China or overseas. The system takes account of the salary levels available to overseas employees should they choose to move to another overseas company and other external factors. Thus, for example, Chinese supervisors may be paid less than their foreign subordinates. One senior Lenovo executive has said that, while executives in China may not be as well paid as their global peers, "they have the most room for development. . . . [Their] privileges are in opportunities, rather than compensation and benefits."[13]

Summary

For global firms, cultural differences are a factor that deserves a great deal of attention. Universal core values should be established and implemented internally to bridge cultural differences and to unify a workforce drawn from a variety of cultural backgrounds and management styles. If neglected, these differences can become problematic and may even lead to the failure of an international M&A. Chinese firms going global must know their objective in seeking M&A and must have solid management systems and corporate cultures in order to integrate their operations successfully. It is incumbent upon senior executives to give the lead in meeting cultural challenges and building universal core values applicable across the expanded organization. Corporate culture can only become ingrained in the company when it is integrated into decision-making, business management, and the daily behavior of executives and employees. Globalization is not a solo performance by the CEO; it is a chorus of the whole company. A core value upheld by each and every one in the company accelerates the journey toward globalization.

Endnotes

1. Li Guohua and Xie Yanglin, "Underestimated Difficulties —TCL's Acquisition of Alcatel," *China Business Journal*, June 20, 2005.
2. "We've Tried Our Best—An Interview with K. Y. Lee," *China Entrepreneur* 22, 2006: 56. There was only one launch in Germany during the year of integration, which was even slower than before the acquisition. What's more, there were no new jointly developed products.
3. Zhang and Chen, 2005: 189.
4. "National Brand Going Global," *Shenyang Daily*, March 5, 2006.
5. Wang and Zhang, 2006.
6. Niu and Yin, 2006: 50.
7. In April 2010, CEO Clemens Joos pointed out that at that moment Lee still had a choice: "The mistakes had been made earlier. Siemens Mobile System did not have an appropriate innovation pipeline, because the investment into next-generation phones (UMTS) was halted before the merger." After the merger, "the innovation backlog had not been worked off: The company just did not live to launch the complete new product range for the Christmas business because Taipei had decided to pull the plug before. The company ran out of time. To kill the business with new products on the shelves for the all-important Christmas season destroyed value and showed insufficient understanding of a big global branded business. Sustaining the Christmas quarter could have limited the damage significantly." According to Joos, the cultural divide was more based on a "fear of things being taken way, the difference was more like 'over-engineering meets over-simplicity', and the dialogue collapsed." For the operational management on both sides, this cultural conflict could not be resolved, and the result was that "speed was crippled and innovation had been delayed due to an overwhelming risk and cost focus in the management preceding the merger." BenQ's limited experience in such matters meant that it was unable "to deal with the new complex and dispersed global sales, marketing, R&D, and manufacturing structure. In conclusion, it was more an issue of company cultures, then of Taiwanese versus German." The end of the deal was unfortunate for both parties: a great deal of corporate value and good will was destroyed. Since that time no other Taiwanese M&A deal has come through in Germany.
8. Shih, 2005: 27.
9. Holt and Wigginton, 2005: 341–43.

10. SAIC president Hu Maoyuan's speech at a Leadership Forum held in Shanghai on March 25, 2006.
11. In an interview with Arthur Yeung.
12. Connie Ma, Trend Micro's Deputy General Manager of Global Human Resource Department, in an interview with Arthur Yeung.
13. Qiao Jiao, Lenovo's vice-president of Global Human Resources, in an interview with Arthur Yeung.

CHAPTER 7

Providing the Right Support: Structuring Global Governance

The essence of building a globalized company is that we should raise funds where the capital is cheapest, produce software where the cost is most advantageous, and sell services where the profit is highest.
Narayana Murthy[1]

Challenges of Global Governance

Business administration becomes increasingly complicated as the company expands its operations and branches all over the world. In addition to recruiting suitably qualified staff as part of their global culture, companies need one more pillar around which to build their organizing capacity—global governance. Suitable employee governance ensures that internal and external resources are fully integrated, guarantees the efficiency and quality of decision-making, and helps ensure that products and services are provided effectively and efficiently in all fields of global operations. It gives full play to the company's organizational capability, rather than simply to individual strengths. Because of traditional culture and their short history of involvement in globalized activities, Chinese firms have two important challenges to overcome in this regard.

Weak integration of global resources

Having fully integrated global resources gives international companies an important competitive edge. Our research has shown that many international firms that operate in China not only have clear advantages in brand management and access to talent and capital, but they are also able to combine internal and external resource advantages at home and abroad by adjusting their organizational structure and support systems in line with industry developments and changes in their own capabilities. They are able to enter local markets by using global resources and incorporate local resources into their structures and systems in a way that strengthens their global competitiveness.

For instance, a number of firms outsource or transfer manufacturing to China, Vietnam and Eastern Europe because of the low-cost purchasing and manufacturing resources there. Many IT companies set up R&D centers in India to make use of low-cost Indian expertise. The three outsourcing giants in the IT field—Infosys Technologies, Tata Consultancy Services, and Wipro Technologies—have advanced to the higher end of the value chain, developing institutes in North America to expand markets there and entering low-cost countries, such as China, to explore new markets and recruit low-cost talent.

An open model for innovation that utilizes external resources (products, intellectual property and talent) is used in companies such as Proctor & Gamble (P&G), IBM, and Eli Lilly. For example, P&G has advanced from a "research and develop" approach to a "connect and develop" approach, using the combined efforts of 7,500 internal employees and 1.5 million experts in its global network to develop new products. Adopting such an approach resulted in significant improvements to its R&D achievements and costs, and to the success rates of its products in just five years.[2]

In knowledge-intensive industries such as consulting and software, the speed at which a company can expand its global activities is dependent on its ability to increase its employees' capabilities and thus establish a global knowledge base that will create more value for its customers. Companies that lack a knowledge-management system tend to rely on individual experts and are often weak in providing speedy solutions tailored to the specific needs of their customers. Companies that rely on the expertise of the few to determine their existence and development face larger operation risks than those who have a wider field of knowledge and skills to call on.

Most Chinese firms lack global operating experience, resource advantages, familiarity with overseas resources, and the ability to integrate them. Some can't even integrate their domestic resources and compete by simply imitating and lowering prices. As China's market opens up and foreign competitors strengthen their ability to integrate Chinese resources, Chinese firms will be at a severe disadvantage if they are confined to the domestic market.

Imbalances in the distribution of power

Successful international companies use advanced control and coordinating systems to manage their overseas subsidiaries and to maintain a balance between global consistency and local responsiveness. But Chinese firms are nurtured in a different cultural and business tradition; they are managed by people, rather than processes. Systems and procedures tend to be neglected by senior managers, who believe they have a better sense of judgment in making decisions. This flexibility can be very efficient when the firm is small and the senior managers have greater vision than the general staff. But as the company expands its scale, product lines and markets overseas, this method will not only harm the quality and speed of decision-making, but can also be challenged by employees who have had experience in working in international companies and can result in conflict, poor cooperation, and inefficiency. It is commonplace for Chinese companies to leave their overseas offices to operate alone. However, if they are to be truly global, they need to achieve a balance between centralized and decentralized power.

Of course, the degree to which these problems arise depends upon the globalization path the company chooses for itself. With strategic alliances, for example, the impact is limited because the two organizations remain independent. However, as we have seen from the examples in earlier chapters, such cooperation provides Chinese companies with a good opportunity to learn unfamiliar management techniques from their alliance partners.

For companies that choose to realize globalization through organic growth, this direction affects the utilization of overseas resources, decision-making in overseas markets and the speed of growth. The biggest advantage of this route is that its step-by-step approach gives companies greater control over risks as they establish overseas bases for manufacturing and R&D.

On the other hand, companies that seek globalization through M&A must have a mature management system and the vision and ability to integrate global resources if they are to realize the synergies they are seeking. While the examples of companies such as CIMC and Wanxiang show what can be achieved when these things are in place, there are many others that have failed precisely because they lacked the necessary experience, culture, and systems to succeed.

To help Chinese firms break through the difficulties, this chapter introduces ways to set up an employee management system that can support their globalization strategy through the design of their organizational structure, and through striking a balance between the centralization and decentralization of power.

Common Global Structure

The organizational structure of a company provides a skeleton or thought process showing how its overall tasks are divided into manageable chunks to be performed by people in different departments, functions, and levels. Based on their assigned tasks, goals, and responsibilities are to be defined, and decision rights and resources assigned accordingly. As the company globalizes, its organizational structure becomes even more complex in order to deal with assigned tasks to be performed by departments or units in different parts of the world. The beginning of the globalization process typically begins with the setting up of an international/overseas business department to take care of business activities outside the company's home country. As overseas sales increase, and the number of markets and product categories proliferates, international business activities can no longer be contained within a department and need to be integrated into the company's overall structure. The most common global organizational structures are established along the dimensions of functions, product lines, regions, or customer groups. Some of these structures are introduced briefly below.

Global functional structure

This function-oriented organizational structure (see Figure 7.1) is appropriate when a company engages in a single-product business

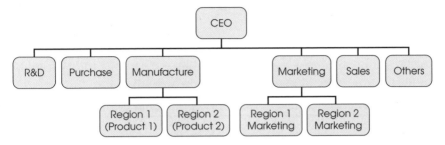

Figure 7.1   Company Organized on Global Functional Structure

or highly-related businesses. It can then divide its business activities based on different functional specializations (such as research and development, purchase, manufacturing, sales, and so on) and then identify the best regions to perform such functional activities (for example, global R&D centers to be located in U.S., Japan, and Germany; global manufacturing centers to be located in China, and so on). There are several advantages to having a global functional structure. Specialization helps to develop real expertise in each functional area. Also, the best practices in each functional area can be transferred and shared from one region to another. Finally, the company's scarcest resources (perhaps its R&D staff or capital-intensive manufacturing facilities) can be commonly shared to support all regions rather than scattered around in different regions. However, such a structure also presents obvious challenges. As each functional department specializes in its own areas of expertise, a silo mentality may develop, making cross-functional coordination difficult. For example, the development of a new product requires close cooperation between several departments (marketing, R&D, manufacturing, and sales), but it can be difficult for peers operating at the same level to make joint decisions on their own. Eventually, this may need to be resolved at senior management level, slowing down business responsiveness.

Global product business units

This product-oriented organizational structure (see Figure 7.2) is exemplified in companies such as Samsung, Panasonic, and GE, which have multiple and unrelated product businesses. Samsung, for example, is engaged in a variety of products including

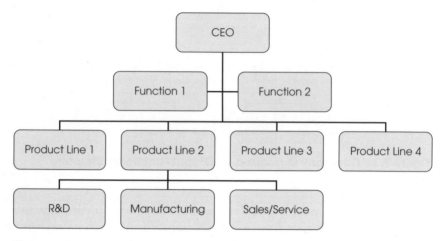

Figure 7.2   Company Organized by Global Product Business Unit

consumer electronics, mobile phones, PCs, and semiconductors. Organizing these on the basis of functional structures is very difficult as the shared functions cannot accommodate the diverse needs of different products well. To ensure responsiveness and speed, all key functions need to be grouped under product business units. Another necessary condition for this to work is that the products offered in each business are quite standardized across regions. In this way, organizing these businesses globally (rather than locally) allows companies to enjoy economies of scale in procurements, product development, and manufacturing as such products can be designed and manufacturing on a massive scale. The shortcomings of global business units are the redundancy of functions and resources within each product business and the difficulty in coming up with a solution across product businesses when customers need products or services beyond the scope of a single business unit.

Regional business unit structure

This region-oriented structure is applicable to companies whose product or service offerings vary substantially from region to region (see Figure 7.3). Such variations are often created as a result of differences in national cultures, levels of economic development, and country-specific laws and regulations such as financial services, professional services, real-estate development, and so on. Organizing

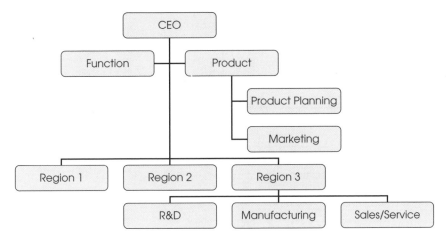

Figure 7.3   Company Organized by Regional Business Unit

these businesses on a regional (rather than a global) basis allows the company to offer products or services adapted to regional differences and responsive to local needs. The major shortcoming of such a structure is that it is difficult to achieve economies of scale in new product development or purchasing because of the idiosyncratic needs of each region. It is also challenging to serve global clients that do business with the company across regions.

Global matrix structure

As their operational scale expands further, companies seek a balance between global scale effects, local responsiveness and knowledge transfer; this results in the need for a global matrix structure such as illustrated in Figure 7.4. This features dual or triple reporting relations: regional managers reporting to regional head and global function head, or regional heads reporting to global function and product business unit.[3] The communication and coordination required by such a system can be both complicated and challenging.

Global Structures Compared

The design of organizational structure is generally influenced by three factors: the founder's managing philosophy, the business environment (politics, technology, and economy), and the company's

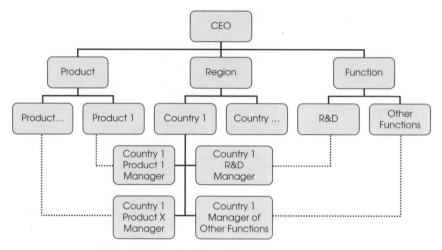

Figure 7.4   The Global Matrix Structure

organizational capabilities. This enables companies within the same industry but established at different times and in different places and with different organizational structures to become leaders in the industry. Philips and Panasonic from the field of electronics, and P&G, Unilever, and L'Oreal from fast-moving consumer goods are good examples of this. European company Philips adopted a region-oriented matrix structure before the 1960s, but resources and power were actually in the charge of branches in different countries because of World War II and tariff barriers. This enabled Philips to meet local needs and attain leadership in the electronics industry. The establishment of the European Common Market and technology development in the 1960s changed the industry rules; the scale effect of manufacturing and the speed of response to the market became key to success. Because its R&D and manufacturing were scattered, Philips faced troubles in cost and launching new products. For instance, while its V2000 video system was technologically better than Sony's Beta and Panasonic's VHS, it abandoned the V2000 because branches in North America chose to sell Panasonic products.[4] Although a newcomer, Panasonic became the leading company because its integrated product structure enabled it to coordinate business direction on a global scale.

Evolution of Global Structures

The focus of organizational structures varies from industry to industry because of their different competitive characteristics. Manufacturing companies generally begin with exports, and then set up sales units overseas. When sales are stable, the company may then set up manufacturing and R&D centers abroad to develop products that meet the needs of the market, to take advantage of local resources, and expand into new markets. Unlike with manufacturing, traditional service industries, such as hotels, banking, and consulting, have to open branches in the areas in which they are to provide services. But thanks to the Internet, the expansion of emerging software and Internet-based industries is much faster than traditional manufacturing and services, and their organizational structures differ accordingly. For instance, Alibaba is located in China to provide services globally. Trend Micro, because of the nature of its business as an anti-virus software company, also had to be ready to serve customers globally. Examples from P&G, a long-established, traditional company, and Trend Micro, an emerging software industry, are provided below to illustrate the evolution of organizational structures.

P&G: Restless Self-renewal

With a history stretching back more than 170 years, P&G's organizational structure has changed with the times.

Early "One Country, Two Systems": In its early years, P&G managed its business overseas via its international sales department. As its scale of overseas business increased, product categories proliferated, and differences in customer needs between American and foreign markets became more marked, P&G adopted a "One Country, Two Systems" principle in the 1950s to the 70s. In the U.S., where there was a large homogeneous market and multiple related product lines, P&G was organized by product business unit (for example, personal care products), with brand managers in charge of each product category (different brands of soaps) inside the unit. Brand managers were responsible for the profits and losses of their product categories. They drew upon and shared the same functional resources, such as R&D within their product business units, while these functional departments shared best practices and talent with different brand departments within product business units. However, outside the U.S., P&G adopted regional business units. For example, in Western Europe, its largest overseas market, where there were several languages, cultures, and sets of regulations to contend with, power was decentralized to the regions. Country general managers were responsible for profits and for meeting local market needs using P&G's technologies and marketing skills. Though this served local needs well, it prevented P&G from implementing universal strategies in Europe. In the early 1980s, P&G was operating in 27 countries, and one-quarter of its US$11 billion sales came from markets overseas. The disadvantages were obvious: high-cost and low-reliability caused by non-standardized R&D, design and manufacturing. As a result, a product-oriented organizational structure was adopted in Europe to improve the decision-making process.

Global Matrix Structure: With the development of markets in Japan and developing countries in the late 1980s, the existing structure could no longer support the company in meeting diversified needs and income levels. Therefore, P&G shifted to a global matrix structure that emphasized both global product businesses and global functions, but using regions as the coordinating units to accommodate regional differences and make the vast territory more manageable. In 1995, this structure was introduced to four regions: North America; Latin America; Europe/Middle East/Africa; and Asia, where the regional CEO was responsible for profits. This structure brought many functional advantages, promoting the accumulation and transfer of knowledge and best practices, standardizing regional operations, and introducing a universal system of purchasing, manufacturing, distribution, information, and finance. The global focus on products greatly accelerated their development, but it also brought some problems. For instance, the objective of the R&D department and the reason for having global product categories was to make technologies and products available to the global market, but regional managers were more concerned with profits in their own regions rather than with the company's strategy. As a result, P&G fell behind its competitors in the global introduction of brands and products.

"Organization 2005": In 1998, P&G announced a six-year reorganization plan to accelerate innovations and their global introuction, to enhance the scale effect, and to reduce costs by increasing the standardization of global procedures. The reorganization was to reduce the number of management levels, lay off 15,000 employees, and replace the matrix structure with seven global business units (GBUs) which were to be responsible for profits and product development, branding, business strategy, and new business development; market development organizations (MDOs), with responsibility for introducing global projects to the regions and helping to make marketing strategies with their understanding of local consumers and retailers; and global business services (GBSs), responsible for costs and charged with standardizing and streamlining internal procedures such as accounting, ordering, and logistics. A global R&D committee was formed to promote the sharing of innovations. Among other structural changes within the organization, the salary system was changed so that a greater proportion of senior managers' salaries were linked to performance and the number of employees to be granted equity options was increased. The initial results, however, were less than satisfactory and in June 2000 A. G. Lafley was appointed CEO. Lafley continued with the general direction taken by "Organization 2005" but took a series of measures to control costs, pool resources, and enhance cooperation between and among the three organizations.

Under Lafley's direction, P&G concentrated on investing in potential top brands globally and, by 2005, it had three global business units: Personal & Beauty, House & Home, and Gillette.

The company set about strengthening cooperation between the three units by creating new positions and changing the indices used for assessing their performance. Although cost remained the major assessment index for business services, business units, and market development, organizations were measured by their customer services.

"Mutual interdependency is a way of life" became one of P&G's principles and was implemented at every level of the company. Lafley eliminated the executives' parking privileges and removed walls in the senior executives' offices so that everyone worked in an open space.

Not all executives supported this reform. By the latter half of 2005, only 10 out of 35 top executives remained in P&G. But the company insisted on internal promotion to ensure the long-term nature of its reforms. In 2003, P&G outsourced some of its business services (to the value of US$4.2 billion) to HP and IBM, which helped the company not only to focus on core business and cut costs, but also to build the ability of the business units in integrating acquired firms such as Gillette.

From 2002, the company maintained fast growth, despite spending less in capital investment and R&D. With lower costs and more flexibility, the speed at which new global products were introduced was shortened from four years to 18 months by 2003. By 2006, there were 22 brands with sales of more than US$2 billion each. The company's sales in 16 regions and 10 biggest retailers increased by an average of 9 percent in four years, while its cost-to-sales ratio was lower than its competitors.

As a company operating within traditional industries, P&G's continuous success has been achieved through self-renewal and an ability to change organizational structure in accordance with its needs at different phases of its development and in response to changes in its competitive environment. Moreover, as the ups and downs of "Organization 2005" prove, changing organizational structure is not simply a matter of redrawing the organizational chart. Rather, the company had to grasp both hard factors (department setup, appointments, and performance-management system) and soft factors (corporate culture, persistence, and the example set by its senior executives) while balancing short-term performance and long-term strategy. This is a highly time- and energy-consuming task, but the benefit is remarkable. Chinese firms that are becoming globalized must be prepared to work on a long-term project instead of a crash restructuring.

Unlike traditional industries, Trend Micro has had a global vision since its inception. In order to make full use of resources everywhere and serve the global market, it uses a unique "transnational" organizational structure, as outlined below.

Transnational Trend Micro

BusinessWeek refers to Trend Micro as a "transnational company," because it is not based in any one country, but has its heads of different functions distributed globally. This unique model was formed in accordance with the resource advantages the company established for itself in a variety of locations (see Table 7.1).

Table 7.1   Trend Micro's transnational model

Country	Center	Resource Advantage
Japan	Finance Center	Stable and cheap funding
U.S.	Marketing Center	Talent and technology
Mainland China/Taiwan	R&D Center	Abundance of R&D talent
Philippines	24-hour Customer-service Center	English-speaking, service-minded staff
Germany	European Headquarters	Easy cooperation with large companies that are strict with quality and are willing to retain long-term business relations to test product and obtain feedback

This organizational structure has two major advantages: first, it makes full use of advantageous resources all over the world; second, as senior executives are located in different regions, they know the local market well enough to put this knowledge together when making joint decisions. Though Trend Micro's model uses global resources effectively and is sensitive to local markets, it poses problems in communications and decision-making because executives and employees are scattered all over the world. The keys to the successful operation of this model are cultural cohesion and a well-ordered communication system.

Prior to 2005, Trend Micro's organizational structure was spread across five regions—the U.S., Japan, Asian Pacific, Europe, and Latin America—and supported by different functions. As the industry developed, the differences between the needs of customers in different regions decreased and those between market segments—big corporations, SMEs, individual, and services—began to be more marked. The company therefore shifted the balance in favor of the latter, which strengthened its responsiveness to customers' needs and the mother company's function and global consistency.

The Trend Micro case is enlightening in two respects: first, it shows the way to enhance competitive edge by using global resources. In some emerging industries (especially in niche markets such as anti-virus software), Chinese companies are not far behind their foreign counterparts. If they were able to integrate global resources, while taking both visible and invisible costs into consideration when designing their organizational structure, they could be even more competitive. Without these conditions, there is little point in trying to copy Trend Micro's model. Second, like P&G, Trend Micro changes its organizational structure according to need.

Designing Global Structure

Organizational structures should be carefully designed so as to give full play to the company's competitive edge. The flow chart shown in Figure 7.5 outlines the steps involved in the process.

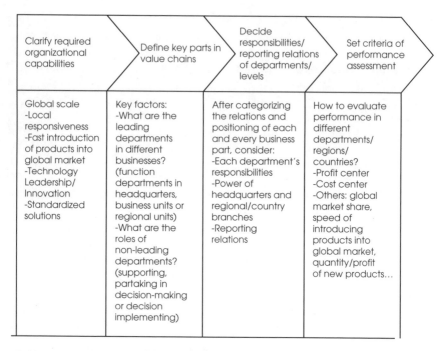

Figure 7.5   Steps in Designing Global Structure

1. **Clarify organizational capabilities:** Based on the industry trends, company strategy, and the resource advantages they have over their major competitors, companies should first clarify what organizational capabilities are critical for them to succeed in the global arena. Are they going to outperform competitors based on low costs, speed of new product introduction, technological leadership, local market responsiveness, or what? What are the two or three most critical capabilities that can help them succeed?

2. **Define key parts in value chain:** Once the critical organizational capabilities are clarified, companies need to decide which units will drive the creation of such capabilities and which will be the supporting units. If the company determines that low cost is critical, then economies of scale in procurement and manufacturing will be critical and these back-end departments will be the driving units, while front-end (customer-facing) units such as sales and services will be supporting units. If technological leadership

is the winning capability, the corporate R&D department will be the driver and other units such as manufacturing or sales will be supporting. If local responsiveness (or customization of products or services to local markets) is critical for success, front-end units such as regional sales and services departments will be critical for success. It is important to determine the relative power of different units.

3. **Determine responsibilities/reporting relations of different departments/levels:** If back-end units are to be the primary drivers for success, companies typically select either a global functional structure (if product businesses are closely related, as in the case of pharmaceutical firms) or global product business units (if product businesses are diverse, as is the case with conglomerates). Decision-making powers will tend to be centralized at headquarters in most cases, including what products to introduce, where to manufacture, what to procure, and so on. If front-end units are the primary drivers for success, regional business units will decide such things as what products to sell, in what quantities, at what prices, and for which clients. In such cases, the role of manufacturing and marketing departments is simply to act as support units. In operations such as this, regional business units is probably the most logical design structure to adopt.

4. **Set criteria for performance assessment:** Based on the respective responsibilities and authority of each unit (global functional departments at headquarters, global product business units or regional business units), the last step is to assign accountabilities for the respective units. What criteria of performance assessment will be used to assess whether the units are performing what they are supposed to perform? Which units are the profit centers (typically the primary driving units) and which units are the cost centers (typically the supporting units)?

To Centralize or Decentralize? A Balancing Act

Large organization have to decide which functions are to be centralized within headquarters, and which are to be decentralized to regions and countries to ensure that the company's strategy and policies are carried out consistently. The respective advantages and disadvantages attaching to centralization and decentralization are set out in Table 7.2.

Table 7.2 Power structures compared

	Centralized	Decentralized
Advantages	Ensures: Implementation of company strategy Centralized allocation of key resources Scale effect Globally consistent operations	Meets local needs Allows fast decision-making Fosters entrepreneurial spirit among executives at branches
Disadvantages	Inefficiency in: Meeting local needs Making speedy local decisions Inspiring entrepreneurial spirit among executives at branches	Inconsistent operation and direction in branches Lack of scale effect

There are three factors that influence how a company organizes the centralization/decentralization of power within its organizational structure:

1. **Product characteristics and company strategy:** Where products are relatively standardized (as with B2B products like machinery or containers) with small regional variations, the centralization of R&D, purchasing and manufacturing brings scale and cost advantages. In the case of products with large regional variations (consumer products such as foods and domestic appliances), decentralization of power is a better choice to strengthen the company's core competitive edge in meeting varied needs. Note, though, that products are not invariable and are becoming increasingly standardized with changes in technology, politics and culture.

2. **Types of function:** Management of back-end activities such as finance, branding, supply chain, and human resources are generally centralized in headquarters to ensure control, efficiency and global consistency. Customer-facing functions (such as marketing, sales, and customer service) are decentralized to enable timely and targeted responses to local needs. The R&D function can be partly centralized (R&D of basic/core technologies) and partly decentralized

(applied/non-core technologies) to branches or segment markets, according to local market needs. As to manufacturing, costs (both manufacturing and transportation costs) and delivery speed in different markets are the key concerns to ensure both efficiency and timely responses. Therefore, non-bulky, high-value products (such as semiconductors) are usually centralized in global manufacturing facilities, while bulky, low-value products (such as cement, or beverage bottling) are usually decentralized close to markets.

3. **Management heritage:** This includes corporate history and culture. European multinational companies started their expansion overseas in the 1920s and 30s.[5] Because of increased tariffs, discriminatory laws and difficulties in transportation and communications, these companies had no choice but to establish local factories. Branches generally operated on their own because headquarters had limited control over them other than in finance. In the 1950s and 60s, American multinational companies enjoyed advantages in both communication technology and more sophisticated management know-how. They were willing to decentralize power while simultaneously managing their overseas operations through standardized procedures and functional experts at headquarters. In the 1970s came Japanese companies that centralized control of R&D, purchasing and manufacturing to ensure cost and quality advantages.

The global business environment is in a state of dynamic change and there is no universal model for determining the ideal distribution of power within organizations. As with organizational structure, the centralization and decentralization of power should be decided according to specific needs of locality and time.

CIMC, for example, developed a group management system that requires consistency of ideas, planning and framework. Control of strategy, purchasing, finance and marketing is centralized at the group's headquarters to ensure consistency of direction within the group, to obtain low-cost raw materials and capital, and to prevent subsidiaries from engaging in meaningless competition. Manufacturing and R&D are decentralized to take full advantage of geographical and human-resource advantages available in different localities. The general manager and finance manager in each subsidiary are deployed from within the group corporation.

In the early stages of its development into a globalized company, Trend Micro allowed a variation of product positioning, marketing strategy, name, and packaging. Because the leaders of its branches in Germany, France, Italy, and Brazil showed the necessary entrepreneurial spirit, the company decentralized management to them to encourage growth in regional markets. When Trend Micro ended its strategic alliance with Intel and was to be listed in Japan, global branding became the priority. The first step in this direction was the establishment of a corporate identity system in 1998. After its Japanese listing in 1998, Trend Micro set up marketing headquarters in the United States to enhance globalized marketing, attract talent, and centralize its branding management. In 2002, the company employed Ogilvy to create an advertisement to promote Trend Micro's global brand image. This advertisement introduced Trend Micro's technology, positioning, and values to CEOs and senior executives (not just IT heads or specialists) of its client companies, and won Best Advertisement of the Year awards in both the U.S. and Japan. Trend Micro was recognized as the Best International Brand in Taiwan by Interbrand.

Founded in Taiwan in 1976, Acer was the third-largest computer manufacturer in the world in 2008, having been listed among the 250 most valuable brands in the world the previous year. Such achievements were based on several reforms that the company undertook, the most important of which were "Rebuilding Acer" in 1992 and "Century Transformation" in 2000.[6] These transformations epitomize the benefits to the company that have accrued as a result of being able to adjust its strategy and the balance between centralized and decentralized power in line with changes in the external business environment.

In the early 1990s, PCs were developing fast: operating systems were becoming standardized, both technology and price were changing rapidly, and industry profits were dropping sharply. To make things worse, Acer was facing a record loss (over US$17 million) arising from a failure of overseas investment and regional operation. To address these problems, Stan Shih came up with three innovative business and organizational strategies:

- **21 in 21:** By the twenty-first century, the corporation would be a combination of 21 companies listed in different countries, each mainly held by local shareholders. This strategy would help Acer solve shortages in finance and human resources, and encourage the entrepreneurial spirit in its local partners to use their local channel and market knowledge to promote Acer's growth.

• **Client-server structure:** Each of the 21 subsidiaries would have its specialized business: some would be regional business units responsible for product sales and service; others would be strategic business units manufacturing main units for global markets. These companies would be responsible for their own profits and losses. Though they would regard each other as priority partners, they could outsource their products or services to other companies and thus help maintain their competitiveness.

• **Fast-food model:** Previously, all Acer's computers had been assembled in Taiwan before being delivered all over the world. The problem was that of excessively long lead time that might lead to price changes in key components as a result of the emergence of more advanced technologies. To avoid this risk, Acer followed the fast-food model, in which all components with different degrees of volatility in price were shipped by sea, land, or air to manage the required lead time. However, computers were assembled in local markets once orders were received so that they incorporated the latest technologies at current market prices.

These three measures formed a decentralized management model that enhanced local responsiveness and brought a greater sense of responsibility to local executives that resulted in greatly improved business performance. Acer's sales were increased by 50, 70, and 80 percent respectively in 1993, 1994, and 1995.

By the late 1990s, however, the PC industry was saturated and profit margins were in decline. Stan Shih's three strategies had achieved success but were beginning to become counterproductive. The 21 in 21 strategy had helped with business growth in local markets, but hindered integration of global resources for which it was competing with global competitors like Dell. The client-server structure had worked well for regional business units but presented difficulties in making global strategies. While the fast-food model had engendered 34 assembly factories all over the world, bad storage control and high costs meant that it failed to realize the expected economies of scale. To address these problems, Acer underwent a second transformation in 2000 for which the new strategic themes were simplification, devotion, and vision.

In 2001, Acer was regrouped into three independent corporations: Acer, which was responsible for sales and marketing of Acer-branded products; Wistron, which was responsible for the design and manufacture of PC and IT products for OEM clients; and BenQ, which was responsible for the design, manufacture, and marketing of computing, communications, and consumer-electronics products. Together, these three companies comprise the Pan-Acer Group. In addition, resources were centralized into regions and profitable product lines, while other product lines/regions were either reduced or closed. In accordance with these strategic themes, Acer centralized its purchasing and global logistics activities to enable it to become more responsive to timely regional market feedback. This new strategic direction established a global team to take full advantage of global integration and synergies and to make use of the global resources of value-chain partners by, for example, using other OEM manufacturers to produce Acer products.

To implement these measures, Acer followed three principles: i) "one company," under which it de-listed the 21 companies to ensure its 100 percent ownership; ii) "one brand," which established its exclusive use of the "Acer" brand; and "one team," which brought all management staff into a single global team.

Any strategy, of course, is only as good as the tools used to implement it. In this regard, Acer set up a new management committee, consisting of the CEO and senior executives from business and regional units, to determine such things as global strategy, product combination, brand management, and resource management. Monthly video conferences and quarterly face-to-face conferences are held to make decisions on major issues.

The company's information system was completely overhauled to provide managers with daily global sales data and weekly sales estimates online. Having this information openly available made rapid decision-making easier and increased the cooperation between senior executives.

Under this new regime, employees were posted to different regions on a rotational basis to broaden their horizons by giving them a clearer understanding of business operations in those regions. This also served to enhance cooperation across departments. Having first proved successful in Europe, this system was then introduced to Asia and the United States.

At the same time, the assessment criteria used in the company's remuneration and incentive system were standardized, with bonuses being awarded in the form of Acer's stocks.

From centralization to decentralization, Acer carried out drastic reforms to adjust its internal structures and operations to meet the changing needs of the external business environment. By doing so, the group's senior management team showed that it had the foresight and the skills necessary to put the company back on track.

After 2006, Acer initiated a multi-brand strategy. With the acquisition of Gateway in 2007 and Packard Bell in 2008, the same principles of sourcing were applied, the main goal being to transform the Acer Group from a manufacturing powerhouse to a globally recognized computer brand that provides world-class products and services.

It is evident from these case studies that companies must adjust their systems in line with external market conditions during different phases of their development. Early decentralization may promote rapid business expansion in different markets but, as the company grows, centralization may become necessary when decentralized activities hinder the integration of global resources and the realization of synergies.

Summary

On the long journey from being a domestic leader to being a global one, change is an unchanging theme. In addition to employing the right talent with the right mindset, companies also need to have the right governance system in place. If they are to achieve this and to compete with globalized firms in domestic markets or overseas, Chinese firms must first have a clear understanding of their shortcomings and weaknesses. Management systems that are entirely reliant on individual leadership hamper growth and will jeopardize any company's future.

Successful companies were not born so and are not infallible, but they do share something in common: an awareness of crisis and a willingness to reform themselves to meet the demands of a changing competitive environment. Companies—whether old transnational or emerging companies—thrive through self-discipline and continuous reform and improvement. Their ability to integrate global resources is acquired through making the necessary adjustments from centralization to decentralization, back and forth, in line with strategic considerations. Success in external markets is achieved on the back of internal strength. For Chinese firms seeking to establish themselves in global markets, there is a great deal to be learned from the experience and lessons of those who have already embarked on the journey.

Endnotes

1. The founder of Infosys Technologies, an Indian software and outsourcing company.
2. Huston and Sakkab, 2006.
3. Bartlett, Birkinshaw and Ghoshal, 2005: 361.
4. Ibid.: 373–84.
5. Ibid.: 362–64.
6. These two cases studies are from Shih, Wang, and Yeung, 2006: 201–17; and Stan Shih, "Acer's Two Transformations," *Business Review* (Chinese version), April 2005: 128.

China-rooted Global Outreach

When the world goes flat—and you are feeling flattened—reach for a shovel and dig inside yourself. Don't try to build walls.

Thomas L. Friedman

he path toward globalization has never been easier. The past two decades have seen several Chinese companies step out into the world and compete successfully on the global stage, while others gained nothing but pain for their haste. Globalization is not a riddle—where there's a will, there's a way. As this book has shown, there is much to be learned from the experiences of companies worldwide doing business at home and abroad.

During our research, we analyzed 21 companies, including BenQ, CIMC, CyberLink, Delta Electronics, Evergreen-Marine, Haier, Galanz, Liugong Machinery, Sinosteel, TCL-Thomson, Trend Micro, and the Wanxiang Group. We found that Chinese companies going abroad ranked themselves very highly when asked to make a self-assessment. In principle, the more than 200 high- and middle-level managers who participated in our analysis were confident that they had gathered the right skills to compete globally. However, our overall assessment of the global organizational capabilities of the companies that took part identified three distinct groups: the good (6), the average (8), and the poor (7).

What was remarkable was that the "good" companies were equally strong in all three categories of global organizational capabilities: global leadership, global mindset, and global organizational structure. These companies rated themselves very highly (83 percent) on all three capabilities, and for companies such as Sinosteel, the Wanxiang Group, and Haier, we found this to be the case. They represent the Chinese companies which think they can operate in the global market place. The other groups had a 72 percent (average) and a 59 percent (poor) score and they showed differences between the categories of about 5 percent. Their weakest area was the organizational structure. This leaves companies such as Liugong, TTE, Changhong, Galanz, and CIMC with great room for improvement (see Figure 8.1). The chart scores the self-assessment of the globalization capabilities on a scale from zero to 100 percent, and clearly distinguishes the companies which are more advanced on the globalization path.

On their way to foreign markets the Chinese companies need to establish systems and procedures which make them successful in global and local markets. In our analysis, the good companies demonstrated strong marketing capabilities in two dimensions in that they fulfilled global requirements and adapted to local needs. While they also had appropriate operating systems well in place, and their human-resource systems certainly fulfilled the globalization and localization requirements, all of these companies have

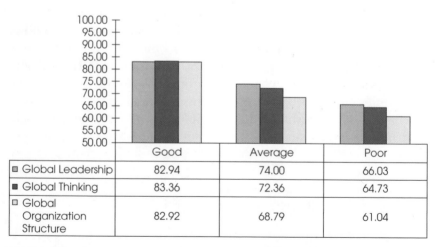

	Good	Average	Poor
▫ Global Leadership	82.94	74.00	66.03
▪ Global Thinking	83.36	72.36	64.73
▫ Global Organization Structure	82.92	68.79	61.04

Figure 8.1   Overall Assessment of Global Organizational Capabilities

room for improvement (see Figure 8.2). About 60 percent of the participating companies estimated their globalization and localization capabilities as insufficient.

The weaker companies judge themselves to be below 70 percent in all categories of systems and procedures. The weakest dimension of all is the human-resource systems, where rapid growth makes doing business difficult for many Chinese companies. Companies which take this issue seriously distinguish themselves from the others and lay the groundwork for prosperous future development. Without doubt, Haier was one of the companies which

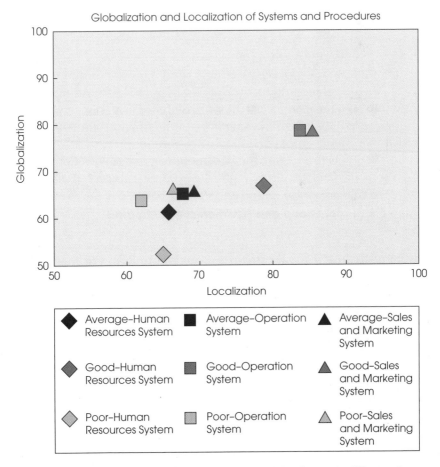

Figure 8.2   Globalization and Localization of Systems and Procedures

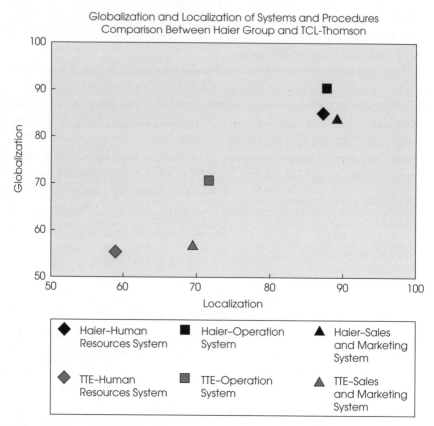

Figure 8.3   Haier Group and TCL-Thomson Compared

distinguished itself in all categories (see Figure 8.3). For many years, it had demonstrated increased performance across many dimensions; even during the financial crises of 2008–09, it was able to increase its revenues by more than 15 percent.

In 2009, Haier reaped net profits of RMB1.149 billion (US$182 million), a 49.64 percent increase on the previous year, and achieved its best company performance ever. In addition, four of the Haier Group's refrigeration technologies received worldwide recognition, being written into international industry standards by the International Electro-technical Commission (IEC). The Group is also recognized as a world-class brand. In June 2009, and for the second consecutive year, it was ranked third among household-appliance companies on the Forbes list of the "World's Most

Reputable Companies." In October 2009, and for the fourth consecutive year, Fortune China ranked Haier first in its list of "The Most Admired Chinese Companies."

In contrast, TCL went through a very difficult time. In 2007, it had to resolve difficulties associated with its acquisition of the Thomson subsidiary in France, which ended in structured insolvency. Our analysis showed that TCL rated poorly, particularly in regard to its human-resource system, where no other company had such low indicators. However, since then TCL has achieved a turnaround and continues to improve steadily. In 2009, it reported increased profits and revenues. Its global market share for TVs grew to 5.7 percent (placing it in fifth position) as a result of the huge increase in demand for low-end LCD TVs in the United States and the emerging markets over the previous year. In mainland China, it is again the leading TV manufacturer. For the coming years, the company sees more growth opportunities arising from the replacement cycle of conventional TVs (CRT) and is committed to improve its internal processes and procedures.

The following general information gleaned from the experiences outlined in earlier chapters may prove useful for Chinese companies as they set about globalizing their activities.

Practical, Confident and Clear-Minded

As latecomers onto the stage of globalization, Chinese firms are disadvantaged in a broad range of areas: talent, capital, brands, technology and management. Because the Chinese market is now open to foreign companies, they also have to contend with sophisticated global-level competition on their own doorstep. However, as the successful globalization of Japanese and Korean firms has clearly demonstrated, these disadvantages need be neither crippling nor permanent. In little more than a decade, Samsung established itself as the leader in DRMA chips, color monitors, and mobile phones; and Toyota replaced GM as the world's largest auto manufacturer in the first quarter of 2007. Analysts who predicted in 2007 that it wouldn't be long before Toyota overtook GM in annual sales,[1] were proved to be correct in 2009.

There are a number of firms from mainland China and Taiwan, including Huawei, ZTE, Haier, Lenovo, BenQ, and Trend Micro, which have made their presence felt on the world stage.

CIMC, ZPMC, and Galanz overcame the disadvantage of being late-comers to establish themselves as leaders in their respective niche markets. In total, 43 Chinese companies have made it onto the Global Fortune 500 list (see Appendix 9).

Know Your Rivals and Yourself

In both domestic and international markets, Chinese firms should be clear about their core competence and their respective advantages and disadvantages vis-à-vis their rivals. This is the only way to define their position and to decide their globalization strategies. Questions they might ask themselves in this regard include:

- What is our positioning: local market competitor, global resource user, global market explorer or global market player?
- What is our objective and strategy both at home and abroad based on our positioning? What are the core functions to be enhanced and strengthened? What are the non-core functions to be outsourced?
- Which markets are for short-term goals? Which ones are for long-term goals? How can we enter and expand markets overseas?
- What resources can be utilized? What resources do we have that can be used as new core competence by cooperating with other companies?

At the very least, Chinese companies should attempt to seize their domestic market. This is the perfect place for learning and improving through competition with foreign competitors, which will prepare them for competition overseas in the future. If they can't compete in their own market, they will face even more pressure in new, foreign markets.

"All roads lead to Rome." Companies can realize globalization via organic growth, strategic alliances or acquisitions. In choosing the path most suited to their current circumstances, they have to consider their capabilities in areas such as risk, speed, control, focus, and organizational management. One thing should be kept in mind throughout—haste makes waste. Although acquisition may seem to offer a shortcut to globalization, this path should only be taken by those who have staff with the necessary skills and experience; an open culture; a well-regulated internal governance system; and an ability to integrate the disparate elements of the companies it acquires. Any company that takes this route must have a clear idea about why it is doing so, what it wants to achieve by doing so, and the problems that it will need to overcome if it is to do so successfully. Most importantly, it has to know when to step away from a deal. A number of Chinese entrepreneurs had to learn this lesson the hard way. We hope that others will learn from their experience, and be more rational when choosing their path to globalization.

Improve Organizational Capability

Companies should know themselves well enough when choosing paths and strategies, and take steps to effect whatever improvements are necessary to realize their goals. They need to:

- overcome traditional perceptions of the "Made in China" label and to establish an excellent brand image.
- be able to attract, cultivate, motivate, and maintain global talent.
- cultivate a corporate culture that is performance-oriented and, at the same time, universal and inclusive.
- utilize global human resources efficiently, balancing the need for centralized/decentralized power structures.

Chinese firms will be able to compete with the giants only when they have resolved these problems. Taking successful global companies as a template for their strategies, they should introduce talent, ideas, and appropriate management tools with an open attitude and set up unique business models to bring their companies onto a new stage. Organizational ability is the key to successful globalization.

Appendix 10 is a questionnaire on the globalization of Chinese firms designed to help companies diagnose and improve their ability through comparison with their counterparts in mainland China, Hong Kong, and Taiwan. In addition, Appendix 11 sets out an action plan to guide companies through three key phases—strategic intention, strategic positioning, and organizational capability—so that they can have a better understanding of their globalization strategies.

Inspiration and Encouragement from the Management Level

Knowing what to do and how to do it is one thing; putting it into action is another matter. It is the responsibility of the management to navigate their companies through the vast ocean of globalization. Senior managers are always vital to the implementation of reforms, particularly in Chinese companies where business tends to be managed by people rather than systems and regulations. To turn a blueprint into reality, the management team should take the lead in incorporating their resolutions into decision-making and allocating the necessary resources and time to the task. Senior managers are required to be critical of their own achievements, open to new knowledge and concepts, and capable of communicating and cooperating with staff from a wide variety of backgrounds. Leading by example is undeniably the most effective strategy for bringing about change. Only when the management team is committed will the employees be convinced that globalization is a worthwhile objective and be willing to identify with this vision.

Rather than being restricted by their current limitations, Chinese companies should root themselves in the domestic market and make full use of the resources available to them. They should develop a global vision to explore the markets abroad, integrate overseas resources, and turn resource advantages into capability advantages. By doing this, they will be able to move away from being imitators to becoming world-leading innovators. As latecomers, they have the advantage of having many examples to learn from. With the right strategy, more and more Chinese companies will surely become major players in the global market of the future.

Endnote

1. Amy Chozick and Norihiko Shirouzu, "GM Slips into Toyota's Rearview Mirror," *Wall Street Journal*, April 25, 2007.

APPENDIX 1

China National Aviation: A Comprehensive Strategy

The China National Aviation Holding Company came into being in October 2002 when the former Air China combined with China National Aviation Company and China Southwest Airlines. Based on the joint air-transport resources of the three parties, Air China Limited ("Air China") was established on September 30, 2004 as the main air-transport company controlled by the China Aviation Group. After six years of strategy planning and implementation, China National Aviation Holding Company now has eight companies including Air China, which is among the Top 20 airline companies in the world. At the end of 2009, its total assets stood at RMB106 billion (US$15.5 billion), as compared with RMB61.1 billion (US$7.37 billion) at the end of 2002.

Step 1: Expansion

Before the amalgamation in 2002, the outdated state-owned airlines were experiencing heavy losses. Although it was the country's largest air carrier, Air China had a debt-to-asset ratio of 94 percent. China Southwest Airlines' debt-to-asset ratio was as high as 97 percent, while the China National Aviation Company's was 40 percent. Growth was constrained by the stagnant domestic market.

Against this background, the China National Aviation Holding Company focused on expansion after reorganization. Its strategy was to promote integration and go public overseas through expansion and strategic restructuring. With the concept of "alliance-driven development and integration-generated ability" in mind, the Group became a stock-holding company of Shandong Air, which also included 44 companies in Air China and 73 companies in its supporting divisions. In addition, it pushed into aircraft maintenance and insurance through cooperation with Samsung Insurance Co.

Step 2: Reinforcement

China's civil-aviation sector underwent great changes from 2005. Internally, the market, price, investment, and aviation rights were all liberalized. Foreign air companies were allowed into the Chinese market and licensed domestic air companies were allowed to operate China-centered international routes. Further reforms governing oil prices and airport charges were introduced and the industry was opened to fierce competition for markets and suitably talented staff. Externally, the passenger and cargo markets were growing fast, along with the Chinese economy. In September 2004, 27 European countries were added to the list of those with Approved Destination Status, making a total of 55 countries. The growth rates of airlines and flights, city pairs and passenger volumes in China were much higher than the world's average.

With the aim of going public, China National Aviation Holding Company shifted its emphasis to reinforcement. In 2006, it set itself the goal to become the most valuable and profitable air company in China, with high-passenger recognition and global competitiveness. It also set about raising its profitability by improving channels, enhancing its resource integration ability, attracting and training staff, and building its brand profile.

In line with this, it stripped away subsidiaries of little or no relevance to its core businesses and developed air-related businesses—air catering, cargo transport and logistics, and airport management and ground handling—with China Aviation (Group) Co. as the platform. China National Aviation Holding Company also strengthened its involvement in competing for business in global and junction cities. In June 2006, Air China launched the "Star Program" jointly with five listed companies to realize mutual support via equity swaps. As a part of its global strategy, in December 2007 Air China became an official member of the Star Alliance—the largest air alliance in the world—expanding its airline network to cover 853 destinations in 157 countries.

Business travelers account for more than 70 percent of Air China's passengers. In 2009, it had over 10 million frequent flyers, more than any of the other domestic-airline companies. World Brand Lab valued Air China's brand at RMB31.7 billion in 2009 and ranked it at number 25 in the world's top 500. In 2004, China National Aviation Holding Company's profit was 57.6 percent; in 2009, this was expected to exceed 70 percent of the total profit of the sector in China. By the end of 2007, Air China had been profitable for seven consecutive years.

In 2006, Air China's A-shares were listed in China. At the last trading day of 2009, Air China's market cap amounted to RMB118.9 billion (US$17.4 billion).

Step 3: Strategic Focus and Improvement

When Kong Dong took the reins of China National Aviation Holding Company in April 2008, industry profits were in decline because of rising international oil prices. Pointing out that the company's problem was that of poorly coordinated development between Air China and other non-core companies, Kong formulated a new strategy that redefined the group's core and non-core businesses and instituted specialized operations within them.

Under the new arrangements, air travel was to be the main driver of the company's diversified operations; cargo, aircraft maintenance, catering and hospitality, engineering, and financial services were to be supporting activities.

APPENDIX 2

CIMC Realizes Globalization with a National Competitive Edge

Container transport is the most convenient and economical way of delivering goods around the globe. As the global economy becomes increasingly integrated, the container transport business is growing fast.

Founded in Shenzhen in January 1980 with funds provided by The East Asiatic Company and Hong Kong Merchants Holdings, China International Marine Containers (CIMC) was one of the earliest container manufacturers in China.

It was relatively easy for CIMC to enter the industry because many of the patents applicable in the industry had expired.[1] By the early 1990s, however, there were more than 40 container manufacturers in China, only one-third of which were profitable in a market where supply exceeded demand. The profit rate per container had slumped from 30 percent in 1988 to less than 3 percent.

In 1987, when the company was on the verge of bankruptcy as a result of poor management, CIMC was transformed into a joint venture of COSCO (45 percent), China Merchants Holdings (45 percent) and the East Asiatic Company (10 percent).[2] Mai Boliang, who had joined CIMC as a technician, was appointed deputy general manager at the age of 28 and became the general manager four years later. In 1993, CIMC went public and was listed on the Shenzhen Stock Exchange in 1994.[3]

Realizing that cost reduction was the key in this business, Mai succeeded in focusing the company's efforts on cost leadership. By setting cost-oriented targets, CIMC reduced standard-container costs by about half in 1992. Similar effort was put into corresponding cost reductions in the order process, and into design and purchasing activities.

In the early 1990s, the Korean container industry was at the forefront of the globalization of the industry, with a market share of more than 60 percent. In 1991, CIMC's leadership envisioned that China could occupy this position but only when its market share was big enough to influence key clients in the industry. With this in mind, in the early 1990s CIMC set about making a series of acquisitions that would enable this to happen.

CIMC acquired more than 10 of its domestic competitors and by 1996 had overtaken its Korean rivals Hyundai and Jindo as the largest container-manufacturer in the world, with a market share of more than 20 percent. As at September 2009, CIMC had more than 34 container-manufacturing bases[4] in south, east, and northeast China. CIMC's competitive edge is built partly on the fact that it has sited its factories on China's major harbors, which enables its clients to ship their goods conveniently while reducing their transportation costs. Because containers manufactured in mainland China are several hundred dollars cheaper than those in Taiwan and Korea, many factories there and in Japan went out of business. The Asian financial crisis also helped boost China's share of the global container market to 90 percent. CIMC continued to expand rapidly through acquisitions. Marshall W. Meyer and Xiaohui Lu (2004) pointed out that: "The central government did not intervene in CIMC's acquisitions administratively because container manufacturing industries are small and not strategic. Nevertheless, they permitted local governments to intervene and support the company since containers are an export-oriented industry. Three-quarters of CIMC's revenues come from clients outside of Asia."[5] In 2008, the company had more than 100 subsidiaries and some 47,000 staff spread over China, North America, Europe, Asia, and Australia. Economies of scale increasingly reduced unit costs.

The company's sales and assets increased by more than 10 times from 1993 to 2002. By 2008, sales had reached RMB47.3 billion (US$6.3 billion), with a net profit of RMB1.4 billion (US$920 million). However, the global economic crisis hit CIMC hard: its revenues for 2009 were only RMB20.48 billion (US$3 billion), down 57 per cent. Its net profit fell to RMB958.97 million (US$140.4 million), a year-on-year reduction of 31.8 percent.

Today, CIMC's core business is still the manufacturing of containers, but it has expanded its services and special-vehicle and transportation applications. The company supplies the world from its 34 Chinese production bases (see Figure A2.1).

Figure A2.1 Locations of CIMC's Major Businesses and Products

Four Major Businesses

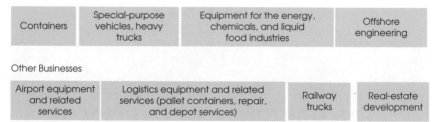

| Containers | Special-purpose vehicles, heavy trucks | Equipment for the energy, chemicals, and liquid food industries | Offshore engineering |

Other Businesses

| Airport equipment and related services | Logistics equipment and related services (pallet containers, repair, and depot services) | Railway trucks | Real-estate development |

Figure A2.2   Composition of CIMC's Business Interests

The vehicle business has also expanded globally. For its road-transportation equipment and services, CIMC has built up 22 production and service stations in North America, Europe, and Asia. With the acquisition of Burg Industries B.V (June 26, 2007) in the Netherlands, it now has interests in the petrochemical, beverage and food transportation businesses. It has also expanded into other manufacturing areas, including offshore-drilling rigs, air-cargo handling, and related air-transportation systems (see Figure A2.2).

Under the guidance of Mai Boliang, CIMC has developed very ambitious goals for the future. Although the global financial crisis has had a big impact, it has not restricted it from becoming a world-class company. Its target for 2012 is to generate revenues of RMB100 billion (US$15 billion) and a net profit of RMB5 billion (US$750 million) and become the global leader in all industries in which it operates.[6] In February 2010, when the global transportation market started to recover, CIMC purchased a 75 percent stake in Friede Goldman United (F&G) from Russia's MNP Group to strengthen its marine-engineering capabilities.

Endnotes

1. Marc Levison, *The Box—How the Shipping Container Made the World Smaller and the World Economy Bigger* (Princeton University Press, 2006).
2. In 2005, COSCO and CMHI became CIMC's largest shareholders, each holding 16.23 percent of stocks. Of the eight directors, there are two from each of these companies; three are independent; and there is one executive director (Mai Boliang).
3. CIMC raised funds of RMB2.47 billion (US$298 million) through stock issuance from 1992–2003.
4. http://www.cimc.com/ir/calendar/abstract/201001/t20100118_4846.shtml
5. Meyer and Lu, 2004: 1:1, 57–86.
6. CIMC Annual Report 2009.

APPENDIX 3

The Utilization of Overseas Resources by CIMC

Having secured a leading position in dry freight, CIMC set its sights on the more technically difficult field of refrigerated ("reefer") containers. Reefer containers have to be built to the highest technical standards to enable them to withstand a whole range of environmental changes from the poles to the equator, as well as the general rigors associated with the container-transport industry.

In the mid-1990s, the overwhelming majority of the world's reefer containers were made of aluminum and the market was dominated by Japanese companies, which held a 95 percent market share. At that time, CIMC made the surprising decision of introducing "sandwich foam" technology from a German company, Graaff, and chose to do business using this non-mainstream technology.

In March 1995, CIMC invested US$50 million to set up Shanghai CIMC Reefer Containers Co., Ltd. (SCRC). Through this move, under which Graaff authorized SCRC to use its 12 key patented technologies in return for a 2 percent shareholding, SCRC gained access to German expertise in the refrigerated container field.

SCRC then spent the equivalent of US$0.49 million to bring in a foam-production machine produced in Germany and, in 1997, assembled a second machine of its own at a greatly reduced cost. In May 2005, Graaff GmbH finally transferred all reefer-container patents to SCRC, allowing the latter to master the whole technical system.

With a huge advantage in price, CIMC rapidly took over the market formerly dominated by Japanese firms. In less than eight years, CIMC's reefer containers became the industry norm. In 2003, more than 70 percent of the world's refrigerated containers were made of steel and were produced using the "sandwich foam" technology.

Following its success in the field of reefer containers, CIMC began to move into the specialist fields of tank and folding containers. In November 2000, CIMC entered into an agreement with the British company UBH International Ltd. to obtain its lightweight-tank manufacturing technology. Fifteen months later, CIMC set up Nantong CIMC Tank Equipment Co., Ltd. (NCTE) to produce stainless-steel tank containers. According to a report by China International Capital Corp., in 2005 NCTE's annual capacity of tank containers would reach 10,000, making it one of the largest producers in the world.[1]

In the folding-container field, CIMC bought 60 percent of the equity of the U.K.-based Clive-Smith Cowley Ltd. (CSC), and thus gained access to key patented technologies such as the Domino flat-rack technology used in some 70 percent of the world's folding-flat-rack market. Before its negotiations with CSC, CIMC had developed its own patented hinge-production plan, which substantially enhanced its bargaining position. Eventually, CSC became a CIMC subsidiary, and its flat-rack production was moved to Guangdong.

Endnote

1. http://www.cimc-tank.com/en/intro.asp

A P P E N D I X

4

ZPMC's Global Strategy

Established in 1992, Shanghai Zhenhua Heavy Industry Co., Ltd. ("ZPMC") (formerly Zhenhua Port Machinery Company) is the world's largest manufacturer of port equipment and large steel structures, with net assets at the end of 2009 totaling US$2.4 billion. That year, with its products available in 73 countries and regions, ZPMC commanded a global market share of almost 78 percent, and achieved an output of RMB28 billion (US$4.1 billion). Figure A4.1 shows the company's recent growth history.

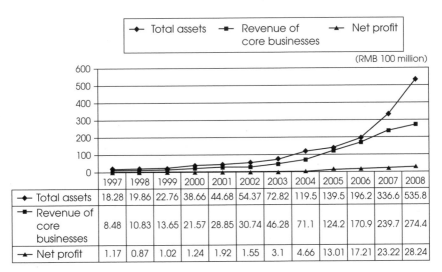

	1997	1998	1999	2000	2001	2002	2003	2004	2005	2006	2007	2008
Total assets	18.28	19.86	22.76	38.66	44.68	54.37	72.82	119.5	139.5	196.2	336.6	535.8
Revenue of core businesses	8.48	10.83	13.65	21.57	28.85	30.74	46.28	71.1	124.2	170.9	239.7	274.4
Net profit	1.17	0.87	1.02	1.24	1.92	1.55	3.1	4.66	13.01	17.21	23.22	28.24

Figure A4.1   ZPMC's Performance, 1997–2008

Built to be Global

Unlike most Chinese firms, which base their globalization on domestic growth, ZPMC was set up with a globalization strategy. ZPMC was founded when its foreign rivals had taken hold of China's ports. Waging price wars on low-end products would have earned it only a small portion of the low-end market and a profit too meager to support technology innovation. However, by going global, disadvantages in technology could be offset by advantages in cost. What's more, average profits generated in the international market were higher than those in the home market, where the cost of technology R&D is much lower than that faced by its international competitors. As long as R&D targets were set correctly, the company would realize its goal of developing technologies independently. Faced with this sink-or-swim situation, ZPMC decided to attempt a breakthrough in international markets and then explore the domestic market with improved capabilities.

Imitating Technologies

Developed countries lose comparative advantage in the manufacture of port machinery because of the labor-intensive nature of the industry, while developing countries are weak in technology and capital. Companies seeking to be industrial leaders have to combine comparative advantage with competitive edge. ZPMC came into being when there was neither a competent Chinese peer nor a production base set up by international competitors. ZPMC squeezed into the international market by adopting a low-price strategy of technology imitation.

In its early stages, ZPMC rented a plant from its shareholder, the Shanghai Heavy Industry Factory, the first port-crane manufacturer in China. ZPMC began by copying the technology being used to install foreign container cranes. By the second year, ZPMC had installed container cranes in Vancouver, on the basis of which it was invited to bid (successfully, as it turned out) for a contract at Miami. The international market's acceptance was a key turning point in ZPMC's global journey. From then on, ZPMC cooperated with industrial giants such as Siemens and ABB in developing its own technology innovations and independent intellectual property to establish itself as a global forerunner in container-crane technology.

Technology Innovation

"ZPMC's growth relies on independent innovation," said its former CEO Guan Tongxian, in our 2007 interview. "ZPMC's core competency lies in technology, independent innovation, and new products. Otherwise, it would be impossible for ZPMC to take hold in international markets, let alone to have a 60 percent market share worldwide . . . Innovation is the only way for companies to survive cut-throat competition."

To encourage this innovation, ZPMC invests 5 percent of its annual output in R&D. Its R&D team comprises more than 600 staff, among whom are 105 master's-degree holders and 153 senior engineers.

ZPMC insists on adopting advanced international standards and patent protection, and on developing products with independent intellectual-property rights. It has conquered more than 20 key technologies, including the world's first double and triple 40-ft container crane, the first super-electronic gantry crane, and the first environment-friendly gantry crane. It has also developed automatic twin-container cranes and straight-moving container cranes using GPS technologies.

Innovative Management

ZPMC believes that innovation depends on the team, which in turn leans on management. To realize its technology targets, it built an R&D system with more than 200 colleges and research institutes at home and abroad. There are headquarters to control operation, design, manufacturing, installation, testing, logistics, and after-sales services, greatly improving its ability to respond to emergencies and risks.

Measures are also in place to motivate ZPMC's employees. These include incentive schemes and a flexible retirement plan designed to retain experienced and competent employees. Awards valued at RMB10 million (US$1.46 million) are given three times a year to recognize technological achievement by engineers and technicians.

Service Foremost

ZPMC's competitiveness is also embodied in its speedy delivery and services. Container cranes demand not only large space and capital but also special handling. The purchase of several special ocean-freight vessels has helped ZPMC to guarantee timely delivery and reduce transportation costs by some 20 percent. Boasting the longest port line and largest capacity in the world, ZPMC is the leading supplier of large-port machinery.

ZPMC is now an international brand enjoying awareness, reputation, and client loyalty all over the world. It wins one-third of all bids it presents—the best result in the industry—and exports container cranes to the U.S. with components made entirely in China. The unflagging reinforcement of its competitive edge and improvements to its capacity for independent innovation and competitiveness in international markets are the company's secret weapons.

In April 2009, ZPMC changed its name from Shanghai Zhenhua Port Machinery Co. to Shanghai Zhenhua Heavy Industry Co., Ltd., reflecting the expansion of the company's business scope. It is predicted that ZPMC will accelerate its push into manufacturing ocean-engineering equipment.

APPENDIX 5

China Mobile: Using Global Capital Resources to Build Value

China Mobile Communications Corporation (China Mobile) utilizes overseas capital to compete in the domestic market. In 1997, China Telecom listed its Guangdong and Zhejiang mobile business on the Hong Kong Stock Exchange and the New York Stock Exchange under the name "China Telecom (HK) Ltd." and raised US$4.22 billion in the process. In 1999, the Ministry of Industry and Information Technology split China Telecom, and China Mobile became one of the spin-offs, operating basic mobile-voice services and value-added services such as data, IP telephone, and multimedia. The company also won the right to operate Internet services and international gateways. China Telecom (HK), a majority-owned subsidiary of China Mobile, changed its name to China Mobile (HK) Ltd. in 2000.

From the end of 1999 to 2004, China Mobile (HK) raised funds from global and domestic capital markets through issuing new shares, debt notes, and strategic subscription agreements. One such agreement was with the Vodafone Group in 2000, when Vodafone acquired new shares of China Mobile for US$2.5 billion. During the same period, China Mobile completed the acquisition of 29 provincial mobile operators, which enabled it to provide services to 31 provinces in China.

At the end of 2004, Wang Jianzhou was appointed general manager of China Mobile. By then, the company, with listed revenues of US$20.75 billion, was ranked at number 242 on the Fortune 500 list, and was sixth among Chinese companies.

The following year was a turning point for China's telecommunication service industry, with the business being opened to foreign investment. Spain's Telefónica acquired a 5 percent share of China Netcom, while Vodafone increased its stake in China Mobile (HK) to 3.27 percent.

Wang Jianzhou recalled: "When I joined the company, our main challenge was whether China Mobile could make further advances and how fast it could maneuver given its size. It was already financially stable. Could it be a tech-led company at the same time?"

In 2005, China Mobile set its new five-year strategy: to become a global leader in the telecommunications industry, to make the leap from good to great, and to modify its strategic positioning from "Mobile Communication Expert" to "Mobile Information Expert." That year, Wang made the book *Good to Great*[1] recommended reading for all China Mobile employees, encouraging innovation and the pursuit of perfection as a core-company value.

China Mobile played a leadership role in the implementation of new strategies and core values in addition to setting up support systems. One such example is that of Xu Long, formerly general manager of China Mobile Zhejiang, who was made general manager of China Mobile Guangdong in mid-2005 when it had over 53 million subscribers—more than double the number served by China Mobile Zhejiang. Additionally, its revenues reached RMB83.52 billion, or 16 percent of the national total.

Based on the group's new strategy and positioning, China Mobile Guangdong established its strategy of "mobile information enabling," focusing on helping people adapt to changes in living and working with mobile-telecommunications networks, technologies or service platforms. The mobile information enabling strategy involved new technologies, new products, and new working modes, all of which posed challenges to employees.

Each month, Xu Long sent a message to employees to communicate the company's strategy, new directions, or his ideas and experiences. In his first month in the post, he sent a message to all mid-level managers and above entitled "Strategy is the root of being big and execution is the root of strength." It included proposals to build a customer-service team and to shift from "looking for customers for our products" to "looking for products for our customers."

Xu also brought home ideas from a trip he made to North America at the end of 2005. He wrote to employees about inspirational innovations being introduced by the likes of Apple, Microsoft, and Warner that enabled telecom carriers to provide telephone, broadband Internet access, and IPTV services through one cable, mobile payment services, and the launch of wireless initiatives that provided content to mobile phones with MP3 and MP4 functions.

In another message, Xu told the story of DeNA, the largest mobile auction site in Japan, which got its start when a Japanese woman set up an auction website to compete with Yahoo! Japan. From humble beginnings, DeNA developed into a public company worth more than ¥1 billion (US$123.7 million).

In 2007, Xu's company messages outlined the latest developments with Apple's iPhone technology, Nokia's camera phones, Microsoft's Windows Mobile 6, and Vodafone's Mobile Plus service. He concluded that these trends would make mobile phones an increasingly important device for Internet access, which would provide telecom carriers with new opportunities.

In addition to encouraging innovation and pursuing perfection, China Mobile's other core values include people-oriented management. Given the company's large customer base, employees are under tremendous pressure, especially those working at call centers. Call-center operators handle an average of one call every two minutes on a wide range of the company's services—which requires that all operators have a firm grasp and in-depth knowledge of all services.

To relieve this pressure, with the aid of external consultants the company established its Employee Assistance Program (EAP) to ease the stress experienced by operators. The program included a hotline for those seeking advice, personal psychological consultations, and training courses in stress management, as well as providing areas for rest and relaxation and free massage services.

In recognition of the importance of its staff, China Mobile Guangdong also developed a range of "Tools" and "Plans" to improve its HR management. These included ways of engaging the capabilities of its workforce more fully in order to build a talent pool that would give it sustainable competitive advantages for the future. Top-performing employees in each of the company's subsidiaries were rotated between regions to give them broader experience of different conditions. This was supplemented with internal training for all subsidiaries across the province.

The company also sharpened its recruitment plans and procedures, gearing them more specifically toward building a pool of talent in, for example, technology, and marketing. These plans also offered diversified compensation and incentive schemes, including subsidies, stock options, and housing allowances for outstanding contributors and key employees.

Endnote

1. James C. Collins, *Good to Great: Why Some Companies Make the Leap . . . and Others Don't* (William Collins: 2001).

APPENDIX 6

Forming Strategic Alliances the Galanz Way

Galanz has always had a clear understanding of its strengths and weaknesses; an understanding that made it possible to consider its position in the global industry. It was aware of the considerable advantages the multinational corporations had in the areas of technology, brand, R&D, and management and so chose to confine itself to the manufacture of a low-value-added mature product—microwave ovens. The reasoning behind this was that multinational corporations would abandon the production of mature products when they realized that they could not compete on cost with Chinese companies such as Galanz. The company's approach was outlined by Yu Yaochang, its executive vice-president:

> First of all, understand yourself, what you can or can't do. If you are not sure of your strengths and weaknesses, you'd better slow down. Identify them clearly first, and do not take the wrong road. Heading in the wrong direction is exhausting and brings no rewards. [Y]ou should make a continuous effort to recognize how much your system can bear in terms of resource allocation, capacity, and other aspects. After understanding all this, you must overcome the difficulties and obstacles ahead, and keep persisting. [H]old on and do not give up in difficult times. You can't win by working only when you want to—you must have diligence.[1]

Galanz clearly understands that its strength lies in manufacturing, where it can make use of a ready and abundant supply of young and relatively cheap workers. The company calculated that, operating on a three-shift system using Chinese workers who are all in their twenties, a production line can run for 160 hours per week. In Europe, by contrast, workers engaged in such traditional industries are generally in their forties and the average working day is only five to six hours, and there are more than 20 days of annual leave. It was clear, then, that Galanz had a clear advantage over its European competitors in cost and productivity. Explaining his company's decision to focus on the manufacturing sector, Galanz president Liang Zhaoxian said:

> After getting a clear understanding that our strength lies in manufacturing, we made efforts to reduce costs, followed the path of large-scale, labor-intensive production, and aimed to be larger, stronger, perfect, and thorough in our field. Galanz focuses solely on manufacturing, and will not make any other choice.[2]

In forming strategic alliances with foreign companies, Galanz was able to offer low-cost manufacturing in exchange for the technology, equipment, and market networks that it lacked. Yu Yaochang explained the company's choice of strategic alliances over M&A:

> What we want is technology, equipment, and talent. We don't need production workers. The integration of Chinese and Western cultures is not so easy. Do we have the ability to integrate Western companies so that they can work for us as Chinese companies do? . . . If the foreign workers strike, what can I do? The unions are very powerful. In addition, their laws make overtime work almost impossible to implement. In addition, how do you digest the labor costs? If they really want an edge, they should move their things to China, where the labor cost is low and productivity is relatively high. We want only things that are more advantageous than ours, and nothing that would be a burden.

Since the 1997 Asian financial crisis, Galanz has gradually convinced European, American, Japanese, and Korean companies to move their production lines to China. In 2008, Galanz had 250 strategic partners, of which more than 80 are world-renowned brands.

Through strategic alliances, Galanz made a rapid and low-cost expansion of its production scale, and captured the domestic and international markets. Galanz's high market share was not always good news, however. The market share of its own brand was once as high as 70 percent in Argentina, but Galanz was forced to withdraw from the market as a result of anti-monopoly charges being brought against it. Therefore, the company had to adopt the strategy of brand transference in its overseas market and serve only as manufacturing partner for its overseas alliance partners.

Endnotes

1. Yaochang Yu in an interview with Professor Arthur Yeung in 2007.
2. Deng and Zhou, 2004.

Trend Micro's Hybrid Team

The anti-viral software industry is, almost by definition, global in nature. It is only natural, then, that Trend Micro has established a multicultural-management team to guide its development in overseas markets. The team comprises executives drawn from the U.S., India, Japan, Germany, and Argentina, as well as from the company's home base in Taiwan. All are vastly experienced global managers. CFO Mahendra Negi, for example, an Indian national who worked in Japan for several years, has experience of other transnational companies, including Merrill Lynch. Zheng Yili, in charge of global product services, is from Taiwan and since joining Trend Micro, has worked in the Philippines, the U.S., and Germany.

The appointment of this multicultural team has seen a shift in the company's decision-making processes. Originally, all decisions were made by the company's founders, Steve and Jenny Chang and Eva Chen. However, with this talented team in place, all decisions are made collectively. While opinions may differ and debates may be fierce, the team shares a strong belief in this transnational management approach. With this hybrid team making decisions together, Trend Micro is able to take full advantage of its global resources and market knowledge. So successful is this approach, in fact, that the Harvard Business School uses the company's decision-making process as a case study in transnational management.

Trend Micro's focus on using its global talent resources is also reflected in its organizational structure. For example, the company's global R&D activities are based in Taiwan, while its 24-hour customer-service center is located in the Philippines to take advantage of the large number of English-speaking service staff there. Yet using global resources puts considerable pressure on communications, coordination, management, and control. The fact that Trend Micro has been able to succeed is attributable in no small way to the cooperation and cohesion demonstrated by its senior leadership—factors which Steve Chang makes a point to emphasize in the many meetings, official and unofficial, he has with this management team. Benefiting from their corporate leader's open-mindedness and trust, Trend Micro's hybrid management team has established the company firmly in the global market.

8

Talent Development in the Lenovo Group

Established in 1984, Lenovo provides computer products and services, electronics and information technology. In 2005, it acquired the PC division of IBM with its headquarters in New York. In 2009, Lenovo had a global sales network and 27,000 employees worldwide. Its R&D centers are located in five major cities in China, in Tokyo, and in Raleigh, North Carolina.

Criteria and Procedures for Promotion[1]

Top 100 Talent Pool

Launched in 2005, this project identifies the best middle- and top-level managers from each business department of Lenovo China on the basis of their ability and leadership potential. These talented individuals are given the opportunity to shoulder greater responsibility and enjoy more development opportunities, such as working overseas, special training (for example, a three-month mini-MBA course) and tutoring from international managers. Their performance and ranking in the talent pool is reviewed annually.

Promotion Criteria

Performance is a top priority and a key determinant of promotion in Lenovo. There are different promotion criteria for different levels. The review of new hires focuses on their performance and adaptability to the corporate culture. Those with consistently excellent performance are promoted—in a system known within Lenovo as "racing."

Managers are reviewed in the following four aspects:

- **Performance:** This is the key criterion. Those working directly in profit-generating activities are reviewed annually. Others are assessed on the basis of individual performance and the development of their department in the previous two-year period.
- **Proficiency:** This looks primarily at customer focus, effective execution, personal excellence, and strategic thinking.
- **Potential:** Here, there are detailed indices to review from four angles: motivation (willingness to get things done well), wisdom (swift judgment and decision-making), learning capability, and vision.
- **Professionalism:** This focuses on their work experience in their specialist areas.

Promotion Procedures

Promotion reviews for middle-level and top executives are conducted by the HR department in conjunction with the reviewee's supervisor and the supervisor's peer and supervisor. They assess the reviewee's potential and performance, and discuss possible career paths. To ensure fairness, explicit criteria are formulated by the HR department annually as the objective measurement of each employee's performance.

For each key position within the company, there are one or two people who are nominated as possible successors. Discussions are held annually between the HR department and leadership about people with high potential and their development plan and career path.

Training System

- **New-hire training:** New employees are trained in corporate culture and history.
- **Professional training:** Internal courses taught by Lenovo senior employees.

- **Racing:** Performance-orientated internal competition is an important way of developing new employees.
- **Pre-management training:** Specific training given to potential managers.
- **Post-promotion training:** Courses relevant to the needs of existing managers.
- **On-the-job MBA program:** To encourage senior managers to cultivate their skills.
- **Mini-MBA program:** A three-month training course at China Europe International Business School.
- **Education Week:** Held annually to update knowledge in a particular field or to update staff on developments within the Lenovo group.

Lenovo's practice is typical among Chinese firms in that employees who demonstrate outstanding performance and potential are entitled to quick promotion—which explains why there are many in their early thirties who are in leadership positions.

Since 2005, Lenovo's talent-development system has been strongly influenced by practices within IBM. Opportunities for promotion come along with business growth and can take different forms. Top performers may be rotated within departments or across functions. There are also some cross-regional rotations where staff members from various branches are invited to work at headquarters for a while and then take this experience back with them to the branches.

As part of the company's succession-planning program, high-potential staff are chosen to act as mentors to those further down the management ladder who are on a similar career path. The company also seeks tutors overseas for its Chinese employees.

Participation of Leadership

Lenovo's founder, Liu Chuanzhi, believes that the leadership's top priority is to formulate strategy and to lead teams. Therefore, Lenovo's senior management pays a great deal of attention to staff training activities. In fact, it is estimated that senior executives spend about one-third of their time engaged in talent management and assessment activities, including conducting in-house training courses. This level of engagement is rare among Chinese firms. Regular informal meetings with senior executives and managers over coffee or lunch also give employees the chance to raise questions or discuss company policy. Surveys are conducted among employees on a quarterly basis to assess, among other things, their managers' ability to convey corporate strategy.

Since its establishment, Lenovo has had an instruction culture where supervisors are willing to instruct their subordinates on work, and also to learn from them. It realizes that providing training and greater opportunities for development and promotion not only improves productivity but also engenders greater loyalty among its staff.

Endnote

1. The interview with Lenovo was conducted in China and the criteria and procedures introduced here are limited to Lenovo China only.

APPENDIX 9

Chinese Global Fortune 500 Companies 2008/09

2009 Ranking	2008 Ranking	Company Name	Revenue (US$ million)	Profit (US$ million)
9	16	Sinopec Group	207,814.5	1,961.2
13	25	China National Petroleum Corporation	181,122.6	10,270.8
15	24	State Grid Corporation of China	164,135.9	664.5
92	133	Industrial and Commercial Bank of China	70,567.5	15,948.5
99	148	China Mobile Limited	65,015.1	11,442
109	132	Hon Hai Precision Industry (Foxconn)	61,860.6	1,748.6
125	171	China Construction Bank	57,976.9	13,323.7
133	159	China Life Insurance (Group) Limited	54,534.1	473
145	187	Bank of China	51,317.2	9,260.5
155	223	Agricultural Bank of China	48,063.2	7,406.4
170	257	Sinochem Corporation	44,457.2	672.3
185	226	China Southern Power Grid Co., Ltd.	41,083	560
218	349	Noble Group	36,090.2	577.3

(Continued)

2009 Ranking	2008 Ranking	Company Name	Revenue (US$ million)	Profit (US$ million)
220	259	Baosteel Group Corporation	35,516.6	2,313.8
242	341	China Railway Group Ltd.	33,758.4	160.5
252	356	China Railway Construction Corporation Ltd.	32,538.4	524.3
263	288	China Telecom	31,813.6	−50.6
281	286	Hutchison Whampoa	30,239.6	2,268.5
291	300	Cathay Financial Holdings	29,852.2	−62.6
292	385	China State Construction Eng. Corp. Ltd.	29,806.7	350.2
306	324	Chinese Petroleum	28,451.9	−3,823.8
318	409	China National Offshore Oil Corporation (CNOOC)	28,027.4	4816.4
323	395	Formosa Petrochemical Co.	27,769.3	481.9
327	405	China Ocean Shipping (Group) Company (COSCO)	27,430.3	1892.8
331	412	China Minemetals Corporation	26,667.2	542.2
335	398	China National Cereals, Oils and Foodstuffs Corp. (COFCO)	26,445.6	500.9
341	426	Chian Communications Construction Company Ltd.	25,982.8	601.8
342	344	Quanta Computer Corp. Ltd.	25,966.7	641.6
359	373	ShangHai Automotive Industry Corporation (Group)	24,882.2	52.9
372		Sinosteel Corporation	24,163.6	155.9
375		He Bei Steel Group	24,033.7	129.7
380	480	China Metallurgical Group Corp.	23,767.3	413.6
385	303	China FAW Group Co.	23,664.4	555.8
411	437	Jardine Matheson	22,362	666
415		China International Trust and Investment Corporation	22,229.1	2050.2
419		China United Telecommunications Corporation Ltd.	21,980.6	2,840.5

425		China Huaneng Group (CHNG)	21,780.7	−512.6
426		China Aviation Industry Corporation	21,737.5	568.4
428		China South Industries Group	21,675.4	296.9
436	363	ASUS Computer Corp. Ltd.	21,173.9	521.9
444		Jiangsu Shagang Group	20,896.9	483.9
494		China Communications Construction Company Ltd.	18,677	4,085.4
499	476	Aluminum Corporation of China Limited (CHALCO)	18,578.7	−744

Source: Global Fortune 500, CNN Money, November 2009

APPENDIX 10

Self-assessment

This questionnaire is designed to help Chinese and other international firms to gain a better understanding of their global competence. Since 2005, more than 200 senior executives from 27 Chinese companies (from mainland China, Hong Kong, and Taiwan) have completed this questionnaire.

This questionnaire evaluates:

- Global leadership
- Employee localization
- Global mindset
- Global organization structure
- Global consistency of systems and procedures
- The extent to which systems and procedures meet local needs

By completing this questionnaire, you can evaluate the status of your company's organizational capability, advantages, and disadvantages, and compare yourself with, and learn from, other companies.

Upon request, we are willing to analyze your questionnaire, provided that you follow up with a feedback report on your company's global organizational capability in comparison to other companies. Our contact:

Centre for Organizational and People Excellence, China Europe International Business School

Tel: 021–28905247

Email (Gary Liu): lgary@ceibs.edu

Questionnaire on the Globalization of Chinese Firms

1. Global Leadership

Please choose the options that best represent your opinion of how the highest level of management in your company/location performs.

The highest level of the managing team of your company/location:	Strongly disagree	Disagree	Neither agree nor disagree	Agree	Strongly agree
1. Understands the global political environment	1	2	3	4	5
2. Is sensitive to changes in the environment that affect the company	1	2	3	4	5
3. Understands global economic problems	1	2	3	4	5
4. Considers business issues from a global angle	1	2	3	4	5
5. Believes local adaptation is indispensable to business globalization	1	2	3	4	5
6. Solves problems by getting information globally	1	2	3	4	5
7. Solves problems by deploying global resources	1	2	3	4	5
8. Provides solutions across borders	1	2	3	4	5
9. Respects cultural differences	1	2	3	4	5
10. Communicates effectively with people of various cultural backgrounds	1	2	3	4	5
11. Solves inter-cultural conflicts effectively	1	2	3	4	5

12. Works well with colleagues from other countries	1	2	3	4	5
13. Communicates regularly with colleagues from other countries	1	2	3	4	5
14. Motivates people from various culture backgrounds	1	2	3	4	5
15. Is respectful and modest	1	2	3	4	5
16. Continues to reform in the face of obstacles	1	2	3	4	5
17. Leads others to overcome fears and a sense of insecurity during reform	1	2	3	4	5
18. Leads others to overcome organizational obstacles during reform	1	2	3	4	5
19. Thinks outside the box to establish new organizational patterns	1	2	3	4	5
20. Is willing to look forward	1	2	3	4	5
21. Is willing to help others to look forward	1	2	3	4	5
22. Generates people's support	1	2	3	4	5
23. Exchanges ideas with colleagues from the same level openly	1	2	3	4	5
24. Exchanges ideas with colleagues from a lower level openly	1	2	3	4	5
25. Thinks multilaterally	1	2	3	4	5
26. Puts itself in others' shoes	1	2	3	4	5
27. Encourages different ideas and opinions	1	2	3	4	5

2. Employee Localization

Please choose the options that in your opinion represent how employees work in your company.

Local employees in your company:	Strongly disagree	Disagree	Neither agree nor disagree	Agree	Strongly agree
28. Have the opportunity to attain senior positions in their countries	1	2	3	4	5
29. Have the opportunity to attain senior positions in their regions (Asia-Pacific, Europe, etc.)	1	2	3	4	5
30. Have the opportunity to attain senior positions globally	1	2	3	4	5
31. Have the opportunity to work globally according to business needs	1	2	3	4	5
32. Have the opportunity to take part in global training or development programs run by your company	1	2	3	4	5

3. Global Mindset

Please choose the options that best represent your opinion of how your company is performing.

Your company:	Strongly disagree	Disagree	Neither agree nor disagree	Agree	Strongly agree
33. Has globally consistent core values	1	2	3	4	5
34. Discusses and improves its core values with managers from all over the world	1	2	3	4	5

35. Clarifies its core values clearly and sets standards	1	2	3	4	5
36. Holds global events to publicize its core values	1	2	3	4	5
37. Informs its employees about its core values and standards	1	2	3	4	5
38. Publicizes its core values regularly (via website, magazines, emails, meetings, etc.)	1	2	3	4	5
39. Has its core values embodied by top managers	1	2	3	4	5
40. Has its core values embodied in senior managers in your location	1	2	3	4	5
41. Is consistent in educating employees in its core values globally	1	2	3	4	5
42. Incorporates its core values in new-hire training	1	2	3	4	5
43. Uses its core values as a benchmark when recruiting	1	2	3	4	5
44. Emphasizes its core values in training and development programs	1	2	3	4	5
45. Includes core values into its performance evaluation	1	2	3	4	5
46. Links its core values with a manager's salary and bonus	1	2	3	4	5
47. Uses the same core values index in different countries	1	2	3	4	5
48. Has managers who balance global consistency and local needs when making decisions	1	2	3	4	5
49. Has people from different countries who work effectively in a multicultural team	1	2	3	4	5

(Continued)

Your company:	Strongly disagree	Disagree	Neither agree nor disagree	Agree	Strongly agree
50. Has people from different countries who trust and respect each other	1	2	3	4	5
51. Solves cultural conflicts and discrepancies in an open and constructive way	1	2	3	4	5
52. Is one in which employees regard global coordination of the company's resources as one of the factors toward success	1	2	3	4	5

4. Global Organization Structure

Please choose the options that best represent your opinion of how your company/business unit is doing.

In your company/business unit:	Strongly disagree	Disagree	Neither agree nor disagree	Agree	Strongly agree
53. The organizational structure supports the company's globalization strategy effectively	1	2	3	4	5
54. The headquarters communicate effectively with its global branches	1	2	3	4	5
55. The headquarters and its branches reach a balance between centralization and decentralization in key fields and procedures (purchasing, R&D, sales, branding, etc.)	1	2	3	4	5

56. Resources are allocated according to relative advantages in different regions/ countries (R&D, manufacturing, purchasing, etc.)	1	2	3	4	5
57. The headquarters' functions are clearly defined and carried out	1	2	3	4	5
58. The headquarters is the center to support and coordinate different countries and products	1	2	3	4	5
In your business unit:					
59. Resources and expertise are effectively deployed globally to solve problems	1	2	3	4	5
60. Local information is provided to the headquarters to support global operations	1	2	3	4	5
61. Local experiences and practices are introduced to the headquarters	1	2	3	4	5

5. Global Consistency

This part is designed to gauge your company's global consistency and local independence with respect to systems and procedures. Please choose the options that best represent your opinion of how your company is doing. 1 means absolute independence of each region/country, while 5 indicates global consistency. The higher the score, the more consistent the systems and procedures are.

Your company has:	Absolutely independent		←→		Globally consistent
62. Strategic planning & budget procedure	1	2	3	4	5
63. R&D planning	1	2	3	4	5

(Continued)

Your company has:	Absolutely independent		↔		Globally consistent
64. Developing planning of new products	1	2	3	4	5
65. Purchasing system	1	2	3	4	5
66. Manufacturing or operations system	1	2	3	4	5
67. Supply chain & storage management system	1	2	3	4	5
68. Branding and sales system	1	2	3	4	5
69. Sales and channel management system	1	2	3	4	5
70. Customer-service system	1	2	3	4	5
71. Finance system	1	2	3	4	5
72. Information system	1	2	3	4	5
73. Information-sharing system	1	2	3	4	5
74. Human-resources management system and practice	1	2	3	4	5
75. Recruitment criteria and procedures	1	2	3	4	5
76. Leadership education/ succession planning	1	2	3	4	5
77. Performance- management criteria and procedures	1	2	3	4	5
78. Design of incentive and welfare system	1	2	3	4	5
79. Entertainment events and tools	1	2	3	4	5

6. The Extent to which Systems and Procedures Meet Local Needs

Please choose the options that best represent your opinion of how different systems and processes meet local market needs. 1 means fails to meet local needs, while 5 means meets local needs well. The higher the score, the better the needs are met.

Your company has:	Fails to meet local needs	←→			Meets local needs well
80. A strategic-planning & budget process	1	2	3	4	5
81. An R&D plan	1	2	3	4	5
82. A development plan for new products	1	2	3	4	5
83. A purchasing system	1	2	3	4	5
84. A manufacturing or operations system	1	2	3	4	5
85. A supply chain & storage-management system	1	2	3	4	5
86. A branding and sales system	1	2	3	4	5
87. A sales and channel-management system	1	2	3	4	5
88. A customer-service system	1	2	3	4	5
89. A finance system	1	2	3	4	5
90. An information system	1	2	3	4	5
91. An information-sharing system	1	2	3	4	5
92. A human-resources management system and practice	1	2	3	4	5
93. Recruitment criteria and procedures	1	2	3	4	5
94. Leadership education/ succession planning	1	2	3	4	5
95. Performance-management criteria and procedures	1	2	3	4	5
96. Designed incentive and welfare systems	1	2	3	4	5
97. Entertainment events and tools	1	2	3	4	5

APPENDIX 11

Action Plan

This action plan is designed for use by firms that are inspired to put their globalization ideas into action. It is intended to be a guide only and can be improved, detailed, altered, and reviewed by senior managers according to the company's circumstances.

1. Define strategic intention behind wanting to globalize: Clarify intention of globalization and define direction, content, and objective in line with the firm's advantages and disadvantages.

Executives' Consensus

Why globalize?

To expand markets

To obtain resources

To create shareholder value

To seek pride

. . .

What is to be globalized?

Capital

R&D

Manufacturing

Sales

Service

. . .

Where to globalize?

Developing/developed countries

Asia/Europe/America. . .

---

2. Define strategic positioning of globalization: Define your company's strategic positioning and focus according to your strategic intention.

Strategic Positioning	Executives' Consensus
What is your company's strategic focus for globalization in the coming three years? - Local market competitor - Global resources user - Global market explorer - Global market player	

3. Evaluate globalization path: Choose one or more paths and try to reduce risks and damage according to what kind of business opportunities or resources the company wants.

	Pluses	Minuses	Executives' Consensus Conclusion
Organic growth	1.	1.	
	2.	2.	
	3.	3.	
	. . .	. . .	
Strategic alliance	1.	1.	
	2.	2.	
	3.	3.	
	. . .	. . .	
M&A	1.	1.	
	2.	2.	
	3.	3.	
	. . .	. . .	

4. Improve employees' globalization abilities: In line with globalization strategy and path, review existing employees' abilities (including senior leaders, middle-level managers, experts/technicians) to ascertain the quality and quantity of employees required, and draw up a detailed action plan.

	Current (quality, quantity)	Ideal (quality, quantity)	Improvement methods (introduction, education, M&A, borrowing)	Action plan (resources needed, person in charge, schedule)
Senior leaders				
Middle-level managers				
Experts/technicians				

5. Improving mindset of globalization: Formulate the ideal corporate culture and corresponding action plan by analyzing the company's existing culture and core values and considering contents to reject, retain, modify, and add.

Existing culture	Ideal culture	Action plan (resources needed, person in charge, schedule)
Core values: 1. 2. 3. . . .	Core values: 1. 2. 3. . . .	Examples set by executives: • decision-making • resource allocation • time allocation • word and action
Other aspects: 1. 2. 3. . . .	Other aspects: 1. 2. 3. . . .	Supporting management system designed and implemented: • communication • recruitment • training • evaluation • incentives • promotion • . . .

6. Adjust employee governance in a globalized way: Adjust the means of managing employees and make corresponding action plans by reviewing the existing organizational structure and the advantages and disadvantages of centralization/decentralization in key systems/procedures.

	Advantages	Disadvantages	Adjustment	Action plan (resources needed, person in charge, schedule)
Existing organizational structure	1. 2. 3. . . .	1. 2. 3. . . .	1. 2. 3. . . .	• Re-design organizational structure • Re-allocate rights, responsibilities and benefits
Centralization/ Decentralization Key systems/ Procedures • Strategic planning • R&D • Purchasing • Manufacturing • Marketing • Branding • Sales • Finance • Human resources • Information systems	1. 2. 3. . . .	1. 2. 3. . . .	1. 2. 3. . . .	

Bibliography

Ashkenas, Ronald N., Lawrence J. DeMonaco, and Suzanne C. Francis. "Making the Deal Real: How GE Capital Integrates Acquisitions." *Harvard Business Review* (Jan/Feb 1998).

Barlett, Christopher A. "GE's Talent Machine: Immelt's Next Step." *Harvard Business School Cases* (August 2006).

Barlett, Christopher A. and Sumantra Ghoshal. "What is a Global Manager?" *Harvard Business Review* (August 2003).

Bian, D., S. Liu, and J. Fernandez. "Sany: Will It Be Sunny in Europe?" EM-Lyon Business School and CEIBS 2008.

Cavusgil, S.T. "On the Internationalization Process of Firms." *European Research* (1980): 8.

Chan, Alan Kam-leung, Gregory K. Clancey, and Hui-Chieh Loy. *Historical Perspectives on East Asian Science, Technology, and Medicine.* Singapore: Singapore University Press, 2001.

Cheng Linfeng, Liu Tao, and Wang Qi. "New Power of Chinese Firms: Finding Commanders Overseas." *China Entrepreneur* 11 (2005).

Chozick, Amy and Norihiko Shirouzu. "GM Slips into Toyota's Rearview Mirror." *Wall Street Journal*, April 25, 2007.

Clissold, Tim. *Mr. China.* New York: Collins, 2004.

Copeland, Lennie and Lewis Griggs. *Going International—How to Make Friends and Deal Effectively in the Global Marketplace.* New York: Plume, 1985.

Crainer, Stuart. *The Management Century.* Hainan Publishing House, 2003.

Dehai Deng and Jian Zhou, *Manufacturing Miracle.* Jiangxi People's Publishing House, 2004.

DiGeorgio, Richard M. "Making Mergers and Acquisitions Work: What We Know and Don't Know." *Journal of Change Management* 3(2) (2002).

D'aveni, Richard A. *Hypercompetition.* New York: Free Press, 1994.

Doz, Yves and C. K. Prahalad. *The Multinational Mission: Balancing Local Demands and Global Vision.* Free Press, 1987.

Doz, Yves L., Jose Santos, and Peter Williamson. *From Global to Metanational.* Boston: HBS Press, 2001: 258.

Fan, Y. "The Globalization of Chinese Brands." *Marketing Intelligence & Planning* 24(4) (2006).

Fairclough, Gordon and Joseph White. "China Car Makers Break Out of the Pack." *Wall Street Journal*, April 28, 2007.

Farrell, Dianna and Andrew J. Grant. "China's Looming Talent Shortage." *The McKinsey Quarterly* 4 (2005)

Farhoomand, A. "Haier: How to Turn a Chinese Household Name into a Global Brand." The Asia Case Research Centre, The University of Hong Kong, 2007.

Gadiesh, Orit, Philip Leung, and Till Vestring. "The Battle for China's Good-Enough Market," *Harvard Business Review* 85(9) (2007): 80–89.

Ghemawat, Panka. *Redefining Global Strategy—Crossing Borders in a World Where Differences Still Matter.* Boston: Harvard Business School Press, 2007.

Ghosen, Carlos. "Creating Value across Cultures: the Renault-Nissan Case." *Entreprises et Histoire* 41 (2005).

Gifford, Rob. *China Road—A Journey into the Future of a Rising Power.* New York: Random House, 2007.

Hamel, G. "Competition for Competence and Inter-partner Learning within International Strategic Alliances." *Strategic Management Journal* 12(1991).

Hamm, Steve and Dexter Roberts. "China's First Global Capitalist." *Business Week* 2 (Chinese Version) (2007).

He Yuxin, Wang Hu, and Bian Caini. "Dongsheng Li's Dunkerque." *Caijing Magazine* 172 (2006).

Hemerling, Jim, David C. Michael, and Holger Michaelis. "How to Acquire Overseas Acquisition Ability." *Caijing Magazine* 172 (2006).

Hollis, N. *The Global Brand.* New York: Palgrave Macmillan, 2008.

Holt, David H. and Karen W. Wigginton. Translated by Wang Xiaolong and Shi Rui, *International Management* 2nd Edition. Tsinghua University Press, 2005.

Hou Weigui. "Opportunities and Challenges in ZTE's Globalization." *IT Time Weekly,* April 5, 2005.

Huston, Larry and Nabil Sakkab. "Connect and Develop: Inside Proctor & Gamble's New Model for Innovation." *Harvard Business Review* (March 2006).

Immelt, Jeffrey R., Vijay Govindarajan, and Chris Trimble. "How GE is Disrupting Itself." Harvard Business Review 87(10) (2009): 56–65.

Ingrassia, Paul. "Daimler-Chrysler Divorce." *Wall Street Journal,* February 21, 2007.

Jacques, Martin. *When China Rules the World: The End of the Western World and the Birth of a New Global Order.* London: Penguin Press, 2009.

Joerres, Jeffrey. "Managing China's Workforce." *Wall Street Journal,* February 12, 2007.

Johnson, H. G. "The Efficiency and Welfare Implications of the International Corporation" in *The International Corporation: A Symposium,* edited by C.P. Kindleberger. Cambridge, Massachusetts: MIT Press, 1970.

Joseph, Ben and Jifu Wang, "From Made in China to Global Chinese Brand." *Journal of International Business and Economics* 8(3) (2008): 155–58.

Kalra, Ajay, Rajiv Surendra, and Kannan Srinivasan. "Response to Competitive Entry: A Rationale for Delayed Defensive Reaction." *Marketing Science* 17(4) (1998).

Kim, W. C. and R. Mauborgne. *Blue Ocean Strategy.* Boston: Harvard Business School Publishing, 2005.

Kirby, T. Y. Manty and F. W. McFarlan. "Li & Fung 2006." *Harvard Business School Case Study* 2007.

Kotler, Philip and Waldemar Pfoertsch. *B2B Brand Management*. New York/ Heidelberg: Springer Publishing, September 2006.

Larcon, Jean-Paul, ed. *Chinese Multinationals*. Singapore: World Scientific Publishing Co. Pte. Ltd., 2009.

Li Guohua and Xie Yanglin. "Slighted Difficulties: TCL's Acquisition of Alcatel." *China Business Journal*, June 20, 2005.

Liu, Shengjun. "Wits and Wisdom in Internationalization." *Southern Weekly*, September 14, 2006.

Meyer, Marshall W., and Xiaohui Lu. "Managing Indefinite Boundaries: The Strategy and Structure of a Chinese Business Firm." *Management and Organization Review* 1 (February 2004).

Hollis, Nigel. *The Global Brand—How to Create and Develop Lasting Brand Value in the World Market*. New York: Martin's Press, 2008.

Niu Wenwen and Yin Sheng. "K.Y. Lee Drew Rein." *Chinese Entepreneur* 22 (2006).

N.N. *30 Reflections of China's 30 Years of Reform 1978–2008*. Beijing: Foreign Languages Press, 2008.

Ohmae, Keniche. *Next Global Stage: The Challenges and Opportunities in Our Borderless World*. Wharton School Publishing, 2005.

———. *The Borderless World*. Harper Paperbacks; revised edition, 1999.

———. *The Mind of the Strategist: The Art of Japanese Business*. McGraw-Hill Professional, 1991.

Palepu, Krishna, Tarun Khanna and Ingrid Vargas. "Haier: Taking a Chinese Company Global." *Harvard Business School Cases* August 25, 2006.

Pascale, Richard, and Anthony Athos. *The Art of Japanese Management*. Penguin, 1982.

Pfoertsch, Waldemar. "China's Multinational Future—China is Building Its Corporate Giants in Many Different Ways." *China International Business* 4 (April 2010).

———. "Truly Made in China: Products Originating and Made in China—Identified as "Time-honored Brands"—Have the Potential to Become World-renowned Products and Lift China from Its Low-cost Mass Manufacturer Status." *BusinessForum China*, February 2010.

Piskorski, Mikolaj Jan and Alessandro L. Spadini. "Procter & Gambler: Organization 2005 (A)" & "Procter & Gambler: Organization 2005 (B)," *Harvard Business School Cases*, November 20, 2006.

Porter, Michael. E. *Can Japanese Compete?* China Citic Press, 2002.

———. *Competition Strategy*. New York: Free Press, 1980.

Prahalad, C. K. and Yves Doz. *The Multinational Mission*. Huaxia Publishing House, 2001.

Qiu Gang, Liyan Xu and Xiaofei Sun. "Assessment of Chinese Companies' Competitiveness." *SERI Quarterly* 2(3) (2009).

Roll, M. *Asian Brand Strategy—How Asia Builds Strong Brands*. New York: Palgrave Macmillan, 2006.

Rothfeder, Jeffrey. "Developing Global Talent." *Chief Executive* 215 (2006).

Shih, Stan. *Rebuilding Acer*. Citic Press, 2005.

Shih, Stan, J. T. Wang, and Arthur Yeung. "Building Global Competitiveness in a Turbulent Environment: Acer's Journey of Transformation" in *Advances in Global Leadership*. Elsevier, 2006.

Simon, Hermann. "Lessons from Germany's Midsize Giants." *Harvard Business Review* (Chinese Version) (May, 2005).

———, *Hidden Champions: Lessons from 500 of the World's Best Unknown Companies*. Xinhua Publisher, 2000.

Sirkin, Harold L., Jim Hemerling, and Arindam K. Bhattacharya. *Globality—Competing with Everyone from Everywhere for Everything*. London: Headline Publishing, 2008.

Sony Information Center. *Sony Memoirs*, Xiyuan Publishing House (March 2000).

Stiglitz, Joseph E. *Making Globalization Work*. New York: W.W. Norton & Company Ltd., 2006.

Terill, Ross. *The New Chinese Empire—and What It Means for the United States*. Basic Books, 2003.

Ulrich, Dave, and Dale Lake. "Organizational Capability: Creating Competitive Advantage." *Academy of Management Executive* 5(1) (1991): 77–92.

Wang Hu "Not Just TCL." *Caijing Magazine* 172 (November 2006).

Wang Hu and Zhang Hao. "The Failure of BenQ-Siemens." *Caijing* 175, December 25, 2006.

Wang Qi, "Stan Shih: Foreign Head is Not Accidental." *Chinese Entrepreneur* 11 (2005).

Wen Liyan. *Human Resource Management in Huawei*. Seasky Publishing House, 2006.

Wernerfelt, B. "A Resource-based View of the Firm." *Strategic Management Journal* 5(2) (1984): 171–80.

Williamson, Peter, and Ming Zeng. *"How to Meet China's Cost Innovation Challenge,"* Ivey Business Journal 72(3) (2008).

———. "Value-for-Money Strategies for Recessionary Times." *Harvard Business Review* 87(3) (2009).

Wolf, Martin. *Why Globalization Works*. New Haven, Conn.: Yale University Press, 2004.

Wu, Fapei, A speech delivered at the Forum on Chinese Firms Going Global held by China Europe International Business School in February 2006.

Wu JingLian. *Understanding and Interpreting Chinese Economic Reform*. Singapore: Thomson/South-western, 2005.

Xin, Katherine, Winter Nie, and Lily Zhang. *Made in China: Secrets of China's Dynamic Entrepreneurs*. John Wiley & Sons, Singapore: 2009.

Xu Yangfan. "The Legend of CIMC." *CEOCIO China*, July 20, 2005.

Yangcheng Evening News, "Pearl River Piano Will Strike a Strong Tone of Global Brand," June 7, 2004: 2.

Yeung, Arthur, Dave Ulrich, Stephen Nason, and Mary Glinow. *Organizational Learning Capability: Generating and Generalizing Ideas with Impact*. Oxford University Press, 1999

Zaheer, S. "Overcoming the Liability of Foreignness." *Academy of Management Journal* 38(2) (1995): 341–63.

Zeng, M. and P. J. Williamson. "The Hidden Dragons." *Harvard Business Review* 81(10) (October 2003): 92–9.

———. *Dragons at Your Door—How Chinese Cost Innovation is Disrupting Global Competition.* Boston: Harvard Business School Press, 2007.

Zhang Mingzheng, and Yizhen Chen. *Irresistible Trend.* Publishing House of Electronics Industry, 2005.

Zhou Linong. *China Business—Environment, Momentum, Strategies, and Prospects.* Singapore: Pearson Education South Asia Pte Ltd., 2006.

Zhu Ling. *China Inc.* Beijing: New World Press, 2009.

Zweig, P. "The Case against Mergers." *Business Week*, October 30, 1995.

Index

Berkeley College